CUTTING-EDGE ARTS, FINE SCIENCES

Dear Emily,

Thank you for giving me my professional start in research and writing long ago. I am happy to join you in the authors' club!

Julie

CUTTING-EDGE ARTS, FINE SCIENCES

INTERDISCIPLINARY APPROACHES TO INNOVATION

JULIE YELLE

NEW DEGREE PRESS

CUTTING-EDGE ARTS, FINE SCIENCES
Interdisciplinary Approaches to Innovation

ISBN   978-1-63676-587-7 *Paperback*
         978-1-63676-215-9 *Kindle Ebook*
         978-1-63676-216-6 *Ebook*

To my family, for the art, music, and dance

CONTENTS

INTRODUCTION

———

Why is origami important for aerospace engineering? How can artisanal weaving save the lives of children with heart defects? What can a choreographer teach the public about the moon landing?

These are questions that, before writing this book, I would not have thought to pose. They would have struck me as complete riddles, as perhaps they seem now to you. This is the power of interdisciplinary collaborations: they help us find solutions to our problems by giving us answers to questions we did not think to ask.

The academic world was where I first glimpsed the power of interdisciplinary collaborations. When I was a graduate student at the University of Texas at Austin, my classmate in the Department of Middle Eastern Studies adapted a methodology from chemistry to analyze classical Arabic grammatical texts.[1] A couple of years later, after I began

———

1   Katie M. Martins, "Vowel Terminology as a Method for Dating Early Arabic Grammatical Texts: A Case Study of Kitāb al-jumal fī l-naḥw" (master's thesis, University of Texas at Austin, 2014).

working as a researcher at the University of Maryland, one of my colleagues contributed to a breakthrough in biological research about DNA using a methodology from linguistics.[2] Meanwhile, I was discovering in my job how my background in social science and linguistics was relevant to the field of computer science.

As someone with broad-ranging passions, I was thrilled to find an opportunity to unite some of my existing interests with a field new to me. Outside of academia, I was also beginning to cross paths with people in the social impact space who were seeking and finding ways to make a difference by connecting the dots between their own disparate interests. When the opportunity to write a book arose, I decided to explore the intersection of science, technology, engineering, and mathematics (STEM) with the arts, seeking to connect my long-held passion for the arts with a rediscovered interest in science and technology—and daring to delve into topics that lie outside of my area of professional specialization.

***

This penchant for cultivating interests in different areas, as it turns out, is a common thread that unites some of the most talented and creative individuals of our time. In her book *Uncommon Genius: How Great Ideas Are Born*, Denise Shekerjian chronicled a series of interviews she conducted with forty MacArthur Fellows—"extraordinarily talented

---

2   Hai H. Le et al., "Tissue Homogeneity Requires Inhibition of Unequal Gene Silencing during Development," *Journal of Cell Biology* 241 no. 3 (2016).

and creative individuals" who were hand-selected to each receive a six-figure, "no-strings-attached award" as an investment in their "originality, insight, and potential."³ Shekerjian talked to fellows in many different disciplines, from renowned paleontologist Dr. Stephen Jay Gould to Nobel Prize–winning poets Derek Walcott and Joseph Brodsky. First noting Gould's "rare gift for seeing the connections between seemingly unrelated things," Shekerjian perceived in multiple fellows a shared quality that is at the heart of creative breakthroughs: willingness and ability to "[break] out of a single frame of reference."⁴

Highly innovative individuals often bask in more than one frame of reference, even when the lasting contributions they put forth into the world are not explicitly cross-disciplinary. Nobel Prize–winning physicist Dr. Richard Feynman was a "surprisingly gifted semi-secret artist," according to Shekerjian.⁵ She also noted that vision scientist Dr. Robert Shapley, "a man who spends a lot of time trying to figure out how the eye perceives shading and color, was very much moved by a show he saw" of Italian baroque artist Michelangelo Merisi da Caravaggio's work.⁶ Dr. Robert Root-Bernstein, professor of physiology at Michigan State University and a MacArthur Fellow himself, led a study of eminent twentieth-century

3   "About MacArthur Fellows Program," MacArthur Foundation, accessed November 17, 2020.

4   Denise Shekerjian, *Uncommon Genius: How Great Ideas Are Born* (New York: Penguin Books, 1991), 6.

5   Ibid.

6   Ibid.

scientists who revealed a striking correlation between scientific success and artistic practice.[7]

Similarly, psychologist Dr. Mihaly Csikszentmihalyi, an expert on creativity who identified and named the mental state of "flow," argued that "creativity generally involves crossing the boundaries of domains, so that a chemist who adopts quantum mechanics from physics and applies it to molecular bonds can make a more substantive contribution to chemistry than one who stays exclusively within the bounds of chemistry."[8]

***

Yet often, the societies in which we live place pressures on us that make it difficult to break out of our primary frames of reference.

The situation is not new. As far back as 1959, English scientist and writer Dr. C. P. Snow was already lamenting the cultural divide separating artistic and scientific spheres of intellectual activity in his famous essay "The Two Cultures." Concerned by a widening gap between the sciences and the humanities, he told a public audience at the University of Cambridge, "Thirty years ago the cultures had long ceased to speak to each other: but at least they managed a kind of frozen smile

---

7   Robert Root-Bernstein and Michele Root-Bernstein, "Artistic Scientists and Scientific Artists: The Link Between Polymathy and Creativity," *Creativity: From Potential to Realization*, ed. Robert. J. Sternberg et al. (Washington, DC: American Psychological Association, 2004), 127–151.

8   Mihaly Csikszentmihalyi, *Creativity: Flow and the Psychology of Discovery and Invention* (New York: Harper Perennial, 1996), 9.

across the gulf. Now the politeness has gone, and they just make faces." Snow attributed the divide between the arts and the sciences in mid-twentieth-century England to a "fanatical belief in educational specialization" and a "tendency to let our social forms crystallize."[9]

What is causing the divide today? "It is an article of faith, among artists and scientists alike, that at some deep level their disciplines share a common ground," David Bayles and Ted Orland wrote in their book *Art & Fear: Observations on the Perils (and Rewards) of Artmaking*.[10] "I think that's true, and the more capable and accomplished the scientist, the more quickly they'll agree," physical and mathematical scientist Dr. Alan Whiting told me. People do not necessarily want to work in silos, he suggested, but "to succeed in academical science and probably in industrial science, you have to concentrate ruthlessly on your career."

Malcom Gladwell, in his book *Outliers: The Story of Success*, would seem to concur. Gladwell's book has popularized the notion, drawn from various studies, that ten thousand hours of practice are required for expert-level mastery in any field, artistic or otherwise.[11]

Csikszentmihalyi has posited that the evolution of culture and the rapid increase in "amounts of information

9   C. P. Snow, "The Two Cultures" (lecture, The University of Cambridge, Cambridge, United Kingdom, May 7, 1959).

10 David Bayles and Ted Orland, *Art & Fear: Observations on the Perils (and Rewards) of Artmaking* (Santa Cruz: Image Continuum Press, 1993), 103.

11 Malcom Gladwell, *Outliers: The Story of Success* (New York: Little, Brown and Company, 2008).

that are constantly being added to domains" have made it "increasingly difficult to master more than one domain of knowledge."[12]

"Nobody knows who the last Renaissance man really was, but sometime after Leonardo da Vinci, it became impossible to learn enough about all of the arts and the sciences to be an expert in more than a small fraction of them," he argued in his book *Creativity: Flow and the Psychology of Discovery and Invention*, which was originally published in 1996.[13]

"Therefore, it follows that as culture evolves, specialized knowledge will be favored over generalized knowledge," he continued, predicting that, over time, "specialists are bound to take over leadership and control of the various institutions of culture."[14]

Indeed, a quarter-century later, Csikszentmihalyi's prediction rings true. The further we advance into the twenty-first century, the more expert-level mastery seems to be a requirement for anyone wishing to succeed in the new millennium's knowledge-based economy. In a 2011 *Harvard Business Review* article, Dr. Thomas W. Malone, Robert Laubacher, and Tammy Johns heralded "the Age of Hyperspecialization." They predicted that, just as the Industrial Age had seen single jobs transformed into many jobs on the assembly line, the rise of knowledge work and communications technology would cause "knowledge-worker jobs" to "atomize into

---

12 Csikszentmihalyi, *Creativity: Flow and the Psychology of Discovery and Invention*, 9.

13 Ibid.

14 Ibid.

complex networks of people all over the world performing highly specialized tasks."[15]

***

When hyperspecialization seems inevitable, exploring outside of one's domain might sound like swimming against the current. "From my observations, it is not widely appreciated that to be usefully cross-disciplinary is harder, sometimes much harder, than to remain specialized," Whiting advised me. "You have to grasp one discipline very well, and another reasonably well, when just staying up to date in one is sometimes all one can do." As for Malone, Laubacher, and Johns, they argued "hyperspecialization pays off" in terms of "quality, speed, and cost" of work.[16]

Yet hyperspecialization, despite its apparent attractiveness and seeming inevitability, is likely to come at a cost. As Csikszentmihalyi warned, the "trend toward specialization" can "easily lead to a cultural fragmentation," potentially leading to a modern-day equivalent of "the biblical story of the building of the Tower of Babel." Even if this trend seems inevitable, Csikszentmihalyi added, it "might be reversible, but only if we make a conscious effort to find an alternative," in what seems to be implicit encouragement to try.[17]

---

15 Thomas W. Malone, Robert Laubacher, and Tammy Johns, "The Big Idea: The Age of Hyperspecialization," *Harvard Business Review*, July–August 2011.

16 Ibid.

17 Csikszentmihalyi, *Creativity: Flow and the Psychology of Discovery and Invention*, 9–10.

It would be to our advantage to try, because significant advancements can be made by leveraging interdisciplinary intersections, such as the ones illustrated in this book. In addition, benefitting from an interdisciplinary outlook does not always require gaining heavily specialized knowledge outside of one's primary field. A little bit of outside knowledge can be enough to make a big difference.

For Apple co-founder Steve Jobs, one calligraphy class was enough to transform the design aesthetics of personal computers. "When we were designing the first Macintosh computer, it all came back to me," Jobs said to graduating students at Stanford University in 2005. "If I had never dropped in on that single course in college, the Mac would have never had multiple typefaces or proportionally spaced fonts."[18]

For mathematician and engineer Dr. Claude Shannon, known as "the father of information theory," a single philosophy course sparked an idea that laid the fundamental groundwork for telecommunications. David Epstein recounts in his book *Range: Why Generalists Triumph in a Specialized World* that, by taking a class in philosophy, Shannon "was exposed to the work of self-taught nineteenth-century English logician George Boole, who assigned a value of one to true statements and zero to false statements and showed that logic problems could be solved like math equations." Shannon brought that knowledge from the realm of philosophy into the field of telecommunications when he went on to work at Bell Telephone Laboratories. "There he recognized that

---

18   Steve Jobs, "Steve Jobs' 2005 Commencement Address," commencement
     address, Stanford University, June 12, 2005, Stanford, CA, transcript and
     YouTube video, 15:04.

he could combine telephone call-routing technology with Boole's logic system to encode and transmit any type of information electronically. It was the fundamental insight on which computers rely," Epstein explained.[19]

***

This book, which focuses on the intersection of STEM and the arts, is filled with more recent stories of innovators who drew ideas and techniques from one discipline into another to arrive at something greater than the sum of its parts. Their stories touch upon dance, visual arts, textile arts, theater, and literature as well as medicine, 3D-printing technology, and mechanical engineering. Their innovations have the potential to shed light on the best practices for breaking out of silos, making meaningful leaps forward in knowledge, and expanding scientific, artistic, and societal possibilities.

While writing this book, I have been asked in curious tones who the intended reader is. I am purposely aiming at a very wide audience. The stories in this book may appeal to scientists, technologists, engineers, and mathematicians as well as dancers, musicians, visual artists, theater professionals, and film artists. Given the positive social impact of the innovations the book features, individuals in the social innovation space will also find it relevant.

On a deeper level, I hope this book will find readership beyond those who have an interest in a subject it touches

---

19 David Epstein, *Range: Why Generalists Triumph in a Specialized World* (New York: Macmillan Publishers, 2019), 33–34.

upon. For example, the book speaks to emerging and experienced professionals seeking to stay relevant to the future of work in a post-digital era. In the years to come, the workforce will increasingly need to be capable of solving complex problems within contexts of unclearly defined rules and changing dynamics. Doing so will require analogical thinking, which, by definition, involves breaking out of a single frame of reference.

This book can also be relevant to anyone who wants to identify an unmet need, or who wants to find a better approach to meeting an already identified need. Anyone who wants to find more innovative, effective ways to create or disseminate knowledge might derive some useful lessons from this book. The book may also be of interest to anyone looking for powerful ways to explore the profundities of human existence.

PART I:

SCIENCES ADVANCE THE ARTS

CHAPTER 1:

TECHNOLOGY INCREASES ARTS ACCESSIBILITY

———

Not every mind or body will experience art the same way. But every mind and body is entitled to the experience.
-THE NATIONAL ENDOWMENT FOR THE ARTS

It is said that invention is born of necessity. What of creativity … an essential prerequisite to invention?

According to visual artist Phil Hansen, "Learning to be creative within the confines of our limitations is the best hope we have to transform ourselves and, collectively, transform our world." In Hansen's case, the limitation he was facing was a hand tremor resulting from permanent nerve damage—in other words, a shake that would never go away. Resigned to abandoning his craft, Hansen thought for years that he would never again produce a piece of art—until a neurologist suggested that he "embrace the shake."[20]

Hansen experimented with reframing his entire approach to art, first embracing the shake and then transcending it. In doing so, he confirmed a novel idea: that embracing a limitation can drive creativity.

"We need to first be limited in order to become limitless," Hansen said in a widely viewed 2013 TEDx Talk, in which he shared the story of his personal struggle and his eureka moment.[21]

"If you treat the problems as possibilities, life will start to dance with you in the most amazing ways."[22]

The beauty of Hansen's story is that, although he first longed to create the kind of art he had made before he developed a tremor, what he got in the end was a more expansive artistic experience for himself and for his audience than he would have created in the absence of that limitation.

When technology is added into the mix, the outcome can be not only a scalable improvement in arts accessibility but also a powerful enhancement of the overall artistic experience.

---

20 Phil Hansen, "Embrace the Shake | Phil Hansen | TED Talks," TED, May 21, 2013, YouTube video, 10:02.
21 Ibid.
22 Ibid.

TOUCHING THE PRADO WITH DIDÚ

Spain's Museo Nacional del Prado has witnessed the power of technology to work around limitations and reach a larger patronage. It became a locus of technology-assisted arts accessibility in 2014, when it unveiled an exhibit called *Touching the Prado.*

Each year, three million visitors flock to the art museum in Madrid, eager to view the world's richest and most comprehensive collection of Spanish paintings.[23] Inside the colonnaded entrance of the museum await iconic works of El Greco, Diego Velázquez, Francisco de Goya, and many other masters of European painting. For those fortunate enough to behold the original masterpieces with their own eyes, the collections are a sumptuous feast of colors, textures, and shapes. Yet for arts and culture aficionados with limited or no eyesight, the exhibits traditionally had little to offer.

Heeding a call to increase overall accessibility, the curators of the Museo del Prado resolved to find a way to do more for potential visitors whose senses of perception do not include sight. Offering audio and braille guides to the works of art seemed an obvious but insufficient option. Determined to offer blind and partially sighted visitors the opportunity to directly experience the masterpieces themselves, the museum invited companies across Spain to pitch their creative solutions to this challenge.

---

23 "The Museo del Prado, Visitors Numbers 2011," Museo del Prado, January 3, 2012, accessed August 24, 2020.

"I know I'm never going to be able to see colors or experience this art the way a sighted person can," admitted Fernández.[28]

Nevertheless, the exhibit gave her a nuanced firsthand appreciation of well-known masterpieces.

"I can feel the texture of the skin, the short beards, and even the look of surprise on the men's mouths," marveled Fernández. "We learned all about the great Spanish artists at school, of course, but it's only now that I can start to understand what made them special in their own unique ways."[29]

Despite the initial successes of the tactile exhibit, making visual art accessible to blind and partially sighted individuals is still in its infancy, and major technical challenges remain.

"If there's too much fine detail in a painting, it would be too hard to convey this using the technology we have, and it would be too much for the reader to take in," Velasco said. "So we had to choose paintings that were artistically significant yet not too detailed. Plus, they had to be the right size. Could you imagine trying to feel your way around *Guernica*?"[30]

Pablo Picasso's enormous *Guernica* has been housed for many years in the Museo Reina Sofia and not the Prado, but, as with highly detailed paintings, mural-sized paintings like *Guernica* would present some real logistical challenges.

28 Hewitt, "Please Touch the Art: 3-D Printing Helps Visually Impaired Appreciate Paintings."
29 Ibid.
30 Ibid.

Also, techniques to differentiate tactile representations of skin, hair, fabric, metals, and glass still need to be developed.

Undeterred by the challenge, Estudios Durero has entered into talks with other institutions in Europe about the possibility of future work in a sustained joint effort between art curators and art technologists to continue improving visual art accessibility.

"This project has been getting quite a bit of attention around Europe and, though I can't say who, we are in talks with other institutions about the possibility of working with them in the future," Velasco hinted. "Most curators are now determined to make art even more accessible, and now we have the technology to do it. Giving blind people the chance to share this part of our culture just seems the right thing to do."[31]

By harnessing the power of technology to make visual art conveyable to a previously unreached audience, the Prado did more than simply make it possible for blind and visually impaired individuals to spend a pleasant day in an art gallery. It also broadened their avenues for understanding and taking pride in Spanish and European culture.

MUSIC: NOT IMPOSSIBLE (M:NI)

Mick Ebeling, the founder and chief executive officer (CEO) of Not Impossible Labs, can attest that embracing possibilities born of a limitation can lead to great innovation. Ebeling's moment of inspiration came to him at a concert when

---

31   Ibid.

some fellow music-lovers unexpectedly caught his attention. Although it is not unusual for people at live concerts to act out of the ordinary, these concertgoers were not starting a mosh pit or pushing their way toward the stage. They were making their way toward the speakers and positioning themselves in front of the vibrations, in order to feel with their bodies what they could not hear with their ears.

Ebeling, ever the entrepreneur, saw a need waiting to be met.

"It's all the low-end sound," he said of the concert speakers. "You don't get the chance to experience any of the fidelity or the acute high ends or other variances that make music magical."[32]

At Not Impossible Labs, Ebeling had been making "technology for the sake of humanity" for a decade, and he knew there must be a way to create a better live music experience for deaf and hard-of-hearing concertgoers. He decided to develop a wearable technology that would use the skin, rather than the ears, as the vehicle of sensory experience.

Ebeling partnered with Daniel Belquer, a professional artist and Not Impossible Lab's director of technology, as well as neuroscientist Dr. David Putrino to bring his vision for a "surround-body" music experience to life.

The first working prototype was a great proof of concept, and the team was thrilled with the initial reaction to it. The

---

32 Jennifer Ouellete, "New Wearable Tech Lets Users Listen to Live Music through Their Skin," Ars Technica, November 25, 2018, accessed August 24, 2020.

beta test with deaf users was so successful the participants were reluctant to give the prototypes back. To perfect the design and technology of the product and bring it to a larger audience, Not Impossible Labs worked closely with engineers from Avnet, a global technology solutions company.

The product they created, called Music: Not Impossible (M:NI), is a vibrotactile, wearable technology. In other words, it allows the wearer to perceive vibration through touch. It is composed of a chest harness with ankle bands and wrist bands that detect and enhance the vibrations of the music. It focuses on translating to the wearer shifts in intensity and amplitude, which the skin is good at detecting. Since the skin can distinguish only a small range of high versus low pitches in comparison to the ears, musical frequencies are de-emphasized.

Not Impossible Labs is clear that the product is meant to enhance the live music experience not only for deaf and hard-of-hearing users but for all concert attendees. That is a lesson Ebeling learned from legendary musical artist Stevie Wonder, with whom he participated on a panel at a disability conference.

When conversations about creating products to serve the deaf community became bogged down by considerations about government mandates, Wonder became frustrated with a focus he viewed as unnecessarily narrow. To set the conversation on a more productive path, he suggested building a product with widespread commercial application for the general population as a more visionary, and more flexible, strategy. Ebeling's director of technology was on board with that strategy too.

"We're not trying to replace music," Belquer said. "We're trying to provide an experience that relates to music. It's less a new technology and more a new form of expression that, instead of going through the ears, goes through the skin. When you feel it, you understand it."[33]

In September 2018, attendees of the Life Is Beautiful Festival, an annual celebration of music and the arts in Las Vegas, were among the first members of the public to get the chance to feel the surround-body experience. The wearable technology was unveiled during National Deaf Awareness Month in a live, private concert featuring the rock band Greta Van Fleet. Two hundred beta testers, including both deaf and hearing music fans, tried out the M:NI kits.

An early tester likened experiencing Beethoven's *Moonlight Sonata* with the kit to "living inside the strings of a piano."[34]

The kits were also a hit among major musical celebrities, including Lady Gaga and Pharrell Williams, who said he had "felt the future" after trying M:NI out.[35]

In developing the product, Not Impossible Labs collaborated with engineering experts from Avnet. Avnet's CEO, Bill Amelio, said, "It was life-changing and exhilarating to

---

33   Ibid.
34   Ibid.
35   Ibid.

see folks from the deaf community enjoying live music, but making this experience happen was a complex problem to solve. Leveraging our strong understanding of technology, design, production, and manufacturing, we worked closely with Not Impossible to guide the process and ensure our collaboration would bring this technology to everyone. And this is only the beginning. We're now working with Not Impossible on additional Vibrotextile products, extending beyond entertainment to therapy, communication, and safety that will improve the lives of many."[36]

Following the initial unveiling, Ebeling expressed his company's intention to release the product publicly in the near future, at a price point that would eventually become within the reach of the average consumer.

"At Not Impossible, we're always about creating accessible solutions for the masses," said Ebeling. "With this project, we'll measure success by the equality we're able to create between the hearing and deaf audiences, through their shared vibratory music experience."[37]

***

If there is one top takeaway from the stories of technology-assisted arts accessibility, it is that exploring new possibilities for artistic engagement through technology is not

---

36 "Avnet and Not Impossible Labs Enable the Deaf to Experience Live Music," Business Wire, September 25, 2018, accessed August 24, 2020.

37 Daniel Bukszpan, "Zappos Wants the Deaf and Hard-of-Hearing to Listen to Music—Here Is the Technology for It," CNBC, October 28, 2018, accessed August 24, 2020.

just good for accommodating a small swath of people with less common user experiences. It can also create exciting new experiences for a general audience, and it can enable shared opportunities for engagement among people whose varying—or nonexistent—experiences in particular settings previously led them to be segmented from one another.

"Limitations may be the most unlikely of places to harness creativity, but perhaps one of the best ways to get ourselves out of ruts, rethink categories, and challenge accepted norms," Hansen told viewers in his closing TEDx Talk remarks.[38]

His thought could not be more on point for initiatives at the vanguard of art and technology. After all, art often challenges societal assumptions and norms through aesthetic means that transcend intellect and logic, grasping at the very core of our being to shake us emotionally into a new view of the world. As for technological advancement, it involves rethinking categories, as what has been proven to be scientifically possible in one context is extended to another context.

---

38   Hansen, "Embrace the Shake | Phil Hansen | TED Talks."

CHAPTER 2:

THE TECHNOLOGY-ASSISTED CREATIVE PROCESS

———

The [art] piece you produce tomorrow will be shaped, purely and simply, by the tools you hold in your hand today. In that sense the history of art is also the history of technology.
-PHOTOGRAPHERS DAVID BAYLES (1952–PRESENT)
AND TED ORLAND (1941–PRESENT)

In their book *Art & Fear: Observations on the Perils (and Rewards) of Artmaking*, David Bayles and Ted Orland acknowledge the role technology has played and continues to play in the creative process throughout the history of art.

"The frescoes of pre-Renaissance Italy, the tempera paintings of Flanders, the *plein [air]* oils of southern France, the acrylics of New York City—each successive technology imparted characteristic color and saturation, brushstroke and texture, sensuality or formality to the art piece," they wrote.[39]

In short, "when new tools appear, new artistic possibilities arise." Yet Bayles and Orland posited that technology has the power to impact not only the form of art, but also its substance: "Your tools do more than just influence the appearance of the resulting art—they basically set limits upon what you can say with an art piece."[40]

In reading their book, I was reminded that one of the world's most influential artistic movements emerged directly in response to a technological innovation:

"A scene painted *from life*, for instance, reveals a world far different from the one painted from memory. This became evident in the 1870s when manufacturers found a way to seal oil colors in collapsible metal-foil tubes, and for the first time, artists working in that medium had the option of leaving the studio and painting with oils directly in the field."[41]

While painting *en plein air* hardly seems a radical move in retrospect, at the time, the idea of leaving the orderly and private environment of a personal studio to paint outside, at the mercy of the elements and sometimes also the bustling crowds, was not at all intuitive—and not every artist opted to do so. The ones who did became known as the Impressionists.

39 David Bayles and Ted Orland, *Art & Fear: Observations on the Perils (and Rewards) of Artmaking* (Santa Cruz: Image Continuum Press, 1993), 58.
40 Ibid.
41 Ibid.

Bayles and Orland's book also offers a reminder that artists are continually presented with new technologies they must evaluate as useful or not to incorporate into their artistic processes: "The dilemma every artist confronts, again and again, is when to stick with familiar tools and materials, and when to reach out and embrace those that offer new possibilities."[42]

The stories that follow are those of artists who have reached out to experiment with new possibilities.

REAL-TIME MOTION CAPTURE OF DANCE CHOREOGRAPHY

In *Art & Fear: Observations on the Perils (and Rewards) of Artmaking*, David Bayles shared a story to which I could distinctly relate and I suspect most, if not all, other artists could as well. He wrote of a "young student" (himself) who, a few months into piano studies, lamented to his teacher, "But I can hear the music so much better in my head than I can get out of my fingers."[43] "What makes you think that ever changes?" the piano master replied, honing into the reality that "vision is always ahead of execution."[44]

I know it to be true that vision precedes execution. Often, my imagination runs much faster than my fingers. Narratives, dialogues, and story lines pop up and float away before I have

---

42 Bayles and Orland, *Art & Fear: Observations on the Perils (and Rewards) of Artmaking*, 59.

43 Bayles and Orland, *Art & Fear: Observations on the Perils (and Rewards) of Artmaking*, 14.

44 Lesia Trubat, "E-TRACES," Behance, November 6, 2014, accessed November 21, 2020.

a chance to put them into writing. On several occasions, my mind's ears have been flooded with the sounds of original symphonies only I can hear, but they fade away before I can set more than a few notes to paper.

At least, when inspiration strikes, I have a form of documentation in mind. When the right words come my way, I know what writing system to use to jot them down or type them up. When a melody pops into my mind, I rely on Western staff notation to capture the first few verses. Even if I had never learned the alphabet or seen a treble clef, I could speak my words aloud or hum my melody into the audio recorder on my smartphone.

As for dance, the means of documentation are more elusive. Yes, there is such a thing as dance notation. There is Labanotation, Banesh Movement Notation, and even the Beauchamp-Feuillet notation commissioned by King Louis XIV of France for seventeenth-century baroque dance. To those who know any of these or other forms of dance notation, *bravissimi*.

Even standardized dance notation sometimes fails to capture every move, though. New York City Ballet soloist Barbara Walczak danced under the direction of the renowned George Balanchine from the 1940s to the 1960s. At that time, she found no conventional term for a particular variant of *attitude à terre* (a standing position used with great frequency in Balanchine's choreography), so she referred to it in her notes as "B+."[45]

---

45 Barbara Walczak, "Doubrovska's Class," *Ballet Review* 43 no. 3 (Fall 2015): 53.

When using standardized dance notation or terminology is not possible, the ubiquity of video camera–equipped smartphones makes filming a viable option. However, because the frame of the camera is limited, some aspects of choreography can get lost. A dancer might move out of the frame, as is often the case when choreography in progress is being filmed from inside a studio. Also, since a video screen is two-dimensional and dance is multidimensional, there can be parts of the recording in which one dancer obscures another.

As a dancer myself, I have run into some of the limitations of the usual ways of documenting choreography. Over the years, I have spent hours working with fellow dancers and choreographers trying to remember the nuances of footwork and the timing of a piece, especially in more fluid dance genres such as modern. This style of dance, as opposed to classical ballet, allows for far more types of movements than could ever fit into a formalized glossary of terminology describing canonical, codified body positions.

As it turns out, there are solutions allowing dancers to combine real-time capture of their choreography with standardized notation.

Lesia Trubat, a product designer from Barcelona, designed and produced a mobile application–enabled pointe shoe wearable, called Electronic Traces (E-TRACES), for real-time recording of ballet choreography. The E-TRACES pointe shoes allow ballet dancers to "recreate their movements in digital pictures" by using the mobile app to "[capture] dance movements and [transform] them into visual sensations," Trubat explained in her online design gallery.[46]

As the dancer's feet make contact with the ground, wearable technology sewn onto the soles and sides of the ballet shoes "record[s] the pressure and movement of the dancer's feet and send[s] a signal to an electronic device." The mobile application then displays the corresponding data graphically, allowing dancers to view all of the movements they have made in video format, extract still images, print them out, and analyze them. "Dancers can interpret their own movements and correct them or compare them with the movements of other dancers," Trubat noted.[47]

"The idea is that this project could be extrapolated to other dance disciplines ([and] even [disciplines] not related to dance, like ... sports)," she explained to HuffPost. "The applications are varied," from "self-learning—or showing the steps in dance classes—to the graphical representation of live performance."[48]

Other emerging technologies track and record motion in similar ways. Motion Bank is a four-year data collection project based in Frankfurt, Germany, that also uses motion-track technology to capture movement and build an open-source dance repository—essentially a digital "library of movement."

---

46   Lesia Trubat, "E-TRACES," Behance, November 6, 2014, accessed November 21, 2020.

47   Ibid.

48   Katherine Brooks, "High-Tech Ballet Shoes Hypnotically Trace the Physical Movement of Dancers' Feet," HuffPost, November 17, 2014, accessed October 10, 2020.

The movements stored in this repository are data points that can be analyzed and visualized through animation, essentially creating digital visual artwork. The ultimate goal of Motion Bank is to allow choreographers and dancers to learn from each other for the overall benefit of dance as an art form.[49]

Apple's ARKit, a framework developers can build upon to create augmented reality (AR) experiences, has also found uses among dancers. Two Seattle-based, salsa-dancing programmers built an app with ARKit called Dance Reality, which lets would-be dancers learn and practice basic steps at home by stepping on brightly colored footprints that appear on the floor and move to the beat.[50] Dance Reality, which was released in 2017 and bills itself as the world's first augmented reality app for learning dance, ranked in the top third of apps globally in terms of number of downloads as of early 2021.[51]

"It's exciting to see more accessible methods of digitally capturing movement," Lauren Bedal, a dancer who works as a human-computer interaction designer at Google, told *Dance* magazine. "For dancers, this unlocks huge opportunities to creatively augment dance performances, view documented dance from all angles, and learn choreography."[52]

---

49   James Carter, "Motion Bank Creates an Archive of Dancer's Movements," VICE, August 13, 2013, accessed January 20, 2021.

50   Dance Reality, accessed January 20, 2021.

51   "Dance Reality," AppTrace, accessed February 16, 2021.

52   Sidney Skybetter, "Meet the Choreographic Interface Designer Who Brings Her Dance Knowledge to Google," *Dance*, September 23, 2020, accessed October 17, 2020.

COMPUTERIZED SONGWRITING

In September 2018, singer and digital storyteller Taryn Southern released *I AM AI*, the first full music album by a solo artist composed and produced using artificial intelligence (AI).

The eight-track album's first single, "Break Free," was released earlier, in August 2017. Within one year, it had more than four million streams, and it rose to number forty-eight on the Mediabase Indicator radio charts in August 2018. The song also attracted media attention, garnering reviews and coverage in *Wired*, *Forbes*, and *Fast Company*.[53]

I AM AI—which Southern composed with a combination of AI software programs, including IBM's Watson Beats, Amper, AIVA, and Google Magenta—is an exploration of human-machine artistic collaboration. The theme of humanity's relationship to technology pervades all of the album tracks.[54]

"Break Free" speaks to the limitations of the human body, expressing a "desire to know what lies [beyond] biological existence" and sensory perception.[55] It is Southern, the human, who wrote the lyrics, setting them to the notation and instrumentation Amper created. Yet if a robot could express its own longings and emotions, what else would it sing about but a wish for a conscious and sentient existence?

---

53 "AI Music," Taryn Southern, accessed November 21, 2020.
54 Ibid.
55 Ibid.

Southern began working on emerging technologies on a virtual reality project with Google through its grant program for artists. While developing a "futuristic world" in virtual reality, she began to wonder, *How can I incorporate other technologies into this world?* While researching artificial intelligence in the art space, she "stumbled upon" AI music generators, "started playing around with them," and became "excited by the kinds of opportunities that they presented for filmmakers."[56]

As a digital personality with half a million subscribers on YouTube, "finding affordable music to license" for her videos "was always a challenge," since she was "pumping out content very, very quickly." In discovering AI-generated music, she initially thought, *This is a really cool tool for content creators and filmmakers to be able to create music on a budget.*[57]

Then, "with some further tinkering," she realized the ability to customize the AI-generation of music was "good enough" that she could actually make an album that would be sufficient "to create a conversation" around what the infusion of emerging technology into the arts "means for the future of music and human creativity."[58]

***

Taryn Southern's experimentation with using software tools to generate new musical compositions was a novel initiative

---

56 Taryn Southern, virtual "Creator Speaker Series" discussion with Eric Koester hosted by the Creator Institute, November 11, 2020.

57 Ibid.

58 Ibid.

with respect to artificial intelligence, but there is another singer-songwriter who brought computer software into his creative process almost a quarter-century earlier: David Bowie, considered one of the most influential musicians of the twentieth century.

Bowie, as his fans will know, had two hallmark characteristics. One was a permanently dilated pupil, which created the illusion his eyes were two different colors. Another was a strikingly otherworldly quality to his song lyrics, which he took great care to create.

Ty Roberts, who was working on creating interactive CD-ROMs for Bowie's *Outside* album in 1994, learned about Bowie's creative approach while observing him in a recording session. In the studio, he saw something peculiar: Bowie was "taking multiple word sources, from the newspaper to hand-written words, cutting them up, throwing them into a hat, and then arranging the fragments on pieces of paper," to "then cross out material that didn't fit to create lines of lyrics."[59]

Known for his "cut-up technique," Bowie regularly engaged in the process of cutting up literary material into words or rephrases and randomly reordering them into new, potentially significant meanings to use in his lyrics.

"If you put three or four disassociated ideas together and create awkward relationships with them, the unconscious

---

59   Matthew Braga, "The Verbasizer was David Bowie's 1995 Lyric-Writing Mac App," VICE, January 11, 2016, accessed August 24, 2020.

intelligence that comes from those pairings is really quite startling sometimes, quite provocative," Bowie discovered.[60]

Have you ever entertained yourself by rearranging a set of word magnets to make poetry on a refrigerator? If so, then you have likely had a similar experience. Physical and mathematical scientist Dr. Alan Whiting pointed out to me the parallel between these popular poetry magnet kits and Bowie's lyric-creation process, noting, "In principle, the options are extremely limited. In practice, they can stimulate the imagination far more than an unlimited blank page."

The cut-up technique itself was not unique to Bowie. He was directly influenced by Beat writer William Burroughs's adaptation of a cut-up technique in the 1960s. Even Burroughs had not invented this approach to creative production. The artist Tristan Tzara, an adherent of the avant-garde Dada movement, had used it as early as the 1920s to write poetry.[61] Yet Bowie was exceptional in his dedication to the technique as a staple of his artistic process.

There is a good reason why no one else used the cut-up technique as regularly as Bowie did. The process of cutting up texts for lyrical inspiration is laborious and time-consuming. What kept Bowie motivated to push through this onerous task?

---

60 "How David Bowie Used 'Cut Ups' to Create Lyrics—BBC News," BBC News, January 11, 2016, YouTube video, 1:34.
61 Austin Kleon, "The Surprisingly Long History of the Cut-Up Technique," Austin Kleon (blog), September 18, 2018, accessed November 21, 2020.

It all stemmed from Bowie's certainty that his lyrics would be his ticket to success. Before David Bowie skyrocketed to worldwide fame, before a punch to the eye gave him his signature look, and even before he was called David Bowie, he was Davy Jones. Intent upon pursuing a musical career from an early age, he performed with a string of different bands before changing his stage name and setting out as a solo artist. He was eager for success, but his initial solo releases failed to hit the charts.[62] He needed a way to differentiate himself, and those unique, fantastical lyrics were it. Indeed, Bowie used the cut-up technique to inspire lyrics for three of his albums, known collectively as the Berlin Trilogy, which are considered to represent some of his best work.[63]

Stepping into that studio and watching Bowie create his lyrics, Roberts saw creative ingenuity hard at work—too hard at work, in fact. Roberts knew there was an easier and more efficient way for Bowie to take the same creative approach. To help speed up Bowie's efforts, Roberts offered to create a software program to automate the randomized lyric-suggestion process.

"It's a program that I've developed with a friend of mine from San Francisco, and it's called the Verbasizer," Bowie announced three years later in Michael Apted's 1997 documentary *Inspirations*, as he demonstrated the automated text randomizer on a Mac computer.[64]

---

62 Adam Sweeting, "David Bowie Obituary," *The Guardian*, January 11, 2016, accessed November 21, 2020.

63 Braga, "The Verbasizer was David Bowie's 1995 Lyric-Writing Mac App."

64 *Inspirations*, directed by Michael Apted (1997; Chicago: Home Vision Entertainment, 2002), DVD.

Before the Verbasizer, Bowie had limited himself to using a relatively small body of text—for example, just one newspaper article, or a single diary entry. With the Verbasizer, Bowie was able to take a much larger corpus of literary material as input and get a much greater volume of output in the form of randomizations he could use as inspiration for song ideas, titles, and lyrics. In this way, the Verbasizer gave Bowie a wealth of material he could take from the computer to the microphone, sometimes in under one minute.

"I'll take articles out of newspapers, poems I've written, pieces of other people's books, and put them all into this little warehouse—this container of information—and then hit the 'Random' button and it'll randomize everything and I'll get reams of pages back out with interesting ideas," Bowie explained in an interview with the British Broadcasting Corporation (BBC).[65]

While the software provided Bowie with the advantage of speed and volume, the magic of his lyric-writing process lay at the intersection of the randomizing power of his technological tool and his emotive capacity as an artist.

"The choices that I now make from this form I can then re-imbue ... with an emotive quality if I want to," Bowie explained in *Inspirations* as he walked viewers through an example of his thought process. Glancing through the Verbasizer output, he continued, "I mean, some of the things I'll empathize with terrifically, and I'll find that even maybe four words in here would—" He stopped himself short as four words grabbed

---

65   "How David Bowie Used 'Cut Ups' to Create Lyrics—BBC News."

hold of him, and he and his musicians soon got to work recording the song that emerged from them.[66]

For Bowie, the Verbasizer was a means of tapping into his subconscious creativity, facilitated by natural language processing technology.

"It's almost like a technological dream in its own way. It creates the images from a dream state without having to go through the boredom of going to sleep all night ... and it will give me access to areas that I wouldn't be thinking about otherwise during the day, because it will prompt ideas and feelings that in the natural course of events I probably would have skirted around or just not been involved in," he explained.[67]

If Bowie had set out to differentiate himself through an unconventional approach to musicianship, the Verbasizer-assisted approach to lyric writing surely helped him meet that goal. Bowie was aware he was taking a risk but could nevertheless not imagine operating differently.

"The way that I work, I will either be extraordinarily accepted, or otherwise I reach a point where I've got seven people listening to what I do," he acknowledged. "I mean, there's never in between, at least! And it's been like that all my life, you know? People have always really accepted what I do or they absolutely sort of push it away from them. And I guess I've gotten used to that, and I guess that's kind of—I guess that's

---

66 *Inspirations.*
67 Ibid.

what I am, you know? Sometimes I'm useful currency and other times I'm not."[68]

Love it or hate it, David Bowie's edgy music earned him the fame he had long sought. He was inducted into the Rock & Roll Hall of Fame in 1996, the year after his first Verbasizer-assisted album was released.[69]

***

Technology offers versatile solutions for artists and art lovers alike to transform, enrich, and amplify the artistic experience. When it is harnessed to boost the process of artistic creation and appreciation, richer art forms, deeper experiences, and broader communities may result.

---

68 Ibid.
69 "David Bowie," Rock & Roll Hall of Fame, accessed November 21, 2020.

CHAPTER 3:

TECHNOLOGY FOR DEMOCRATIZATION OF THE ARTS

———

In the history of art, the work of art is now a social object.

-JIAJIA FEI, DIGITAL STRATEGIST
FOR THE ART WORLD (1987–PRESENT)

The fine arts have long been the privilege of the aristocracy or have been highly stratified. In centuries past, the patron often had as much or more influence on the art than the artist who created it, since in controlling the funding, the commissioning party had the power to determine the content of the art and influence its style.

Yet with the proliferation of digital technologies in recent years, the doors have been opening up to disrupt the hierarchy, changing how artists are funded, what kinds of art they create, and who buys and interacts with their art.

ARTSTECH MEETUP

In the first decade of the twenty-first century, as social media and smartphones were ushering in the shift from the dot-com era to the digital age, leading art galleries were grappling with questions about how to harness the power of these new platforms and devices.

"Around this time, there were a lot of people who were in newly created digital media positions within cultural organizations. ... These were new positions, new roles without precedent, without best practices ... and the landscape was changing really rapidly," New York–based cultural producer Julia Kaganskiy recounted to the host of Art19's *State of the Art* podcast.[70]

This shift in the online landscape coincided with another source of major disruption and uncertainty: the Great Recession. Kaganskiy, who had spent her youth constructing the perfect foundation for her dream career as an arts and culture magazine editor, graduated right at the outset of the global financial crisis that devastated the economy, all while the publishing industry was set into a tailspin. Growing up in New York, she had done everything right: taken classes in drawing, painting, ceramics, and piano; frequented art galleries, ballet performances, and the opera; written for a music magazine throughout high school and college; and branched out from music journalism into covering film, art, and culture. Yet in 2007, despite her bachelor's degree from

---

70 Julia Kaganskiy, "The Art Incubator: Julia Kaganskiy at New Inc," April 19, 2018, in *State of the Art*, produced by ART19, podcast, MP3 audio, 1:30:39.

one of the top journalism programs in the United States, her prospects were looking shaky.[71]

"Well, it looks like that job in journalism is just never going to happen," Kaganskiy told herself. She concluded that she had better find a new career path. Thus, she landed back in New York at a dot-com start-up called Unigo, where she channeled her journalism skills into social media management and content marketing. She found the technology start-up scene to be a "really welcoming and heady space for a twenty-one-[going on] twenty-two-year-old, because as opposed to the media space, which was very hierarchical, very 'pay your dues before anyone's going to pay you any mind,' the tech community was much more open and curious." It made her feel she "could have a hand in helping to build and shape something."[72]

Building and shaping something, as it turns out, was just what she would end up doing. Over time, Kaganskiy began to feel the call to unite her new world with her old one. "There was this great sense of possibility [in the tech community] that I really fell in love with, but after the initial charm wore off, I kept wanting to find a way to connect this back to something that I was really interested in and passionate about," she explained. She wanted to continue using her digital communications skills, but for a purpose greater than promoting online sales. "How can I connect this to something that I can really feel good about?" Kaganskiy asked herself.[73]

---

71   Ibid.
72   Ibid.
73   Ibid.

An insightful friend offered a suggestion that turned the light bulb on over Kaganskiy's head about how to connect her tech skills with her passion for the arts. Famous New York City art galleries and museums such as the Metropolitan Museum of Art or the Museum of Modern Art (MoMA) were certain to be grappling with questions about how to leverage new social media platforms such as Facebook and Twitter. "Maybe you should investigate and see what's happening at this intersection of art and tech!" the friend encouraged her.[74]

Kaganskiy took the suggestion and ran with it. She began researching and writing a blog on which she published case studies about how different museums were using Internet technology. Although she started writing the blog primarily to synthesize her own thought process and educate herself, an audience caught on to her findings.

"I was sharing these articles on Twitter and connecting with various professionals working at this intersection of art and tech on Twitter, people from various museums, places like Lincoln Center [for the Performing Arts], and engaging in this dialogue online," Kaganskiy recounted.[75]

Out of the online dialogue grew an in-person Arts, Culture, and Technology (ArtsTech) meetup in New York that Kaganskiy founded and facilitated as "a way to deepen that research and learn with others." The mission of her meetup was "to democratize the arts" and "to bring art and digital culture closer together." As a robust community of people

---

74 Ibid.
75 Ibid.

interested in the intersection of art and technology regularly gathered, Kaganskiy began to invite thought leaders and highly accomplished professionals to join them. To her great surprise, "amazing speakers" readily accepted the invitations, because the meetup provided them with an ideal forum in which to discuss their work. "I guess I had tapped into a need in the New York City arts and culture space without knowing it," Kaganskiy mused.[76]

In the early years of digital communications, the arts and technology dialogue was a timely one that addressed an emergent priority in the cultural sector. In isolation, digital media specialists in the arts world were "making it up as they went along and figuring things out on the fly," but as a community, they were able to "share best practices, share resources, learn from one another, talk about what they were seeing out in the field, and also to meet in person for the first time."[77]

Indeed, the meetup brought individuals and communities into contact with one another that Kaganskiy was truly surprised had never previously met. "I was bringing together people from this cross-section of art and technology that I thought should be talking to each other, but for whatever reason were kind of siloed," she remarked. The distinct categories of individuals Kaganskiy's meetup united included technologists in the start-up ecosystem who were creating products marketed toward cultural institutions and art lovers, employees of cultural institutions working in technology

76 Ibid.
77 Ibid.

roles, and artists incorporating technology into their art. Intent on having them learn from one another's different perspectives, Kaganskiy chose to organize the meetups such that one representative from each of those categories spoke on a common theme.

"It was a way to … bring these different micro-communities under the banner of art and tech into contact with one another," she explained.[78]

For that reason, the ArtsTech meetup was a valuable networking forum. Kaganskiy reported "careers took off because of access to this community." Even more significantly, the meetup was a catalyst for innovation.

"One of the collaborations that really stands out in my memory is that we had a curator who actually got her start on Tumblr," Kaganskiy shared.[79]

DIGITAL ART AUCTIONS

That curator was Lindsey Howard, the curatorial director of digital art gallery 319 Scholes. Howard recounted in an interview with Complex that Megan Newcome of Phillips auction house and Annie Werner of Tumblr, who had met through the ArtsTech meetup, had "decided that they wanted to collaborate and mix the best of Phillips and the best of Tumblr" by launching a digital art auction. They reached out to Howard to ask if she would curate it. She accepted,

78 Ibid.
79 Ibid.

teaming up with the duo to host the world's first-ever auction of digital art at Phillips in October 2013.[80]

Howard anticipated several novel advantages in holding a digital art auction. She saw it as "a fantastic opportunity" to introduce the work of digital artists to "a broader range of collectors, bring more exposure," and "further the market for this kind of work." She believed that the digital art auction would open doors to "young collectors, new collectors, and people who were learning about [digital art] for the first time." She also saw the auction's potential to show audiences that the digital art would not just amount to "walking in and seeing a bunch of screens."[81]

"About half of the works are screen-based, but there's also textile, sculptures, prints—multiple mediums and multiple outputs for works—that are either made with digital tools or using digital technology as a medium itself," she explained.[82]

Most of all, she viewed the auction as a way to test and shape the future of digital art. One of her team's original goals, she specified, was to connect the tech and start-up communities with digital art for the benefit of the artists. She sought to "potentially create some kind of alignment there for collectorship, patronage, and support," which was especially needed

80 Leigh Silver, "Interview: Lindsay Howard Talks Curating the First Digital Art Auction with Phillips and Tumblr," Complex, October 10, 2013, accessed October 4, 2020.
81 Ibid.
82 Ibid.

at a time when understanding what it meant to own a piece of digital artwork was still crystallizing.[83]

"Everyone should be supporting their own generation's artists, because those are the artists who are making the most sense and helping people understand what's going on in their culture," Howard affirmed.[84]

***

Within only a few years, "digital" began to describe not only the type of artwork up for auction, but also the format of the auction itself, as art-selling and -collecting events moved from in-person venues to virtual platforms.

In a virtual event in August 2020 that she led for fellow Georgetown University alumni (myself included), art advisor Astrid Oviedo Clark discussed how the COVID-19 pandemic had created changes in the selling and collecting of art. Before COVID-19, she explained, art collecting more or less required showing up in person to a gallery, because "there were no prices online," and "people were embarrassed to ask about prices." Yet as in-person events became impossible due to the pandemic, art collection events became digitized.[85]

Art Basel Hong Kong Online, held in March 2020, served as "a test of their new online format," and it was "a resounding

---

83   Ibid.
84   Ibid.
85   Astrid Oviedo Clark, "The World of Art: Navigating and Collecting in Today's Market," virtual presentation and discussion hosted by Georgetown University, August 25, 2020.

success in a couple of ways." First, it attracted a record number of visitors, since it was free, in contrast to the in-person events for which the standard price of a ticket was sixty-five dollars per day. Second, visitors had "twenty-four-hour access" to the art online.[86]

"Immediately, the art became more accessible and more transparent," Clark remarked, explaining that virtual event attendees got unprecedented access to art studios that had previously been unofficially "reserved for the top collectors."[87]

At that time, directors of art galleries, who were laying off much of their staff to devote their funds to their digital teams, were worried they would come up short financially in online auctions. However, revenues through online auctions in fact exceeded projections made for the in-person event. Francis Bacon's *Triptych Inspired by the Oresteia of Aeschylus*, for instance, sold for 84.5 million dollars—well above the anticipated 60 million dollars—in a live-streamed Sotheby's auction.[88]

The positive reception to Art Basel Hong Kong Online and other successful events revealed that the online art world might truly be feasible, said Clark. "It is the same players but an altered marketplace," she explained. "The localized marketplace was growing through new ways to have contact." For example, galleries began offering augmented reality technology that allowed visitors to take an image of a work of

---

86 Ibid.
87 Ibid.
88 Ibid.

art, point their smartphones against the wall, and see what the artwork would look like on the wall before bidding on the art.[89]

***

The COVID-19 pandemic affected not only global art shows but also graduating art students. In March 2020, master of fine arts (MFA) students at San Jose State University's CADRE (Computers in Art, Design, Research, and Education) Laboratory for New Media were experiencing a crisis because their scheduled art shows had to be canceled, leaving them unable to display their final exhibitions. Fellow student Don Hansen—an Internet artist, designer, and new media art researcher based in Oakland, California—began thinking about how to solve that problem in the face of a "complete shutdown of all art spaces."[90]

For "about a year or two," Hansen had been experimenting with three.js open-source software, which is used for 3D rendering in a web browser. As faculty and fellow students began to seriously consider the possibility of participating in online exhibitions, Hansen set out to develop a virtual art space called New Art City.[91]

New Art City is a website, and every show has a unique URL, with no extra software required to experience the shows. "I

---

89 Ibid.
90 "New Paradigms and Spaces for Artistic Expression," Leonardo Art/ Science Evening Rendezvous, virtual presentation and discussion hosted by Stanford University, August 27, 2020.
91 Ibid.

was able to pull in images and put them on these panels, and it actually felt like I was looking at art in this 3D space," Hansen recounted.[92]

"The goals for this project, at a broad level, are to create a space where artists can show work to a worldwide audience, outside of the limitations of physical space," reflected Hansen. Indeed, over the course of five months, from March to August 2020, Hansen and two collaborators hosted seven public exhibitions through New Art City, with more than twenty artists featured in each one, and a total of "6,900 visitors from seventy-seven different countries all over the world."[93]

Accessibility and inclusivity were integral to the format.

"We wanted to build a fully expressive tool for anybody to produce a show, regardless of their technical skill. This is a no-coding-required platform," Hansen explained. "We do conduct our own curation efforts, but it's really about what the community and the public bring to the platform. Our own curation focuses on highlighting people who are underrepresented in the arts or new to the art world altogether."[94]

Hansen stressed that New Art City is not simply an online version of a physical art space:

---

92 Ibid.
93 Ibid.
94 Ibid.

"New Art City is a virtual art space in the sense that it attempts to represent an actual space in the virtual world. It's not really an art gallery, though; it's more of a platform for everybody to create their own shows, so any gallery—any institution, collective, or artist—will be able to launch their own shows on New Art City."[95]

New Art City's configuration as a space in virtual reality, rather than a digital rendering of physical space, is what differentiates it from other virtual galleries:

"Some of the other options in the virtual gallery landscape really mimic the white-walls gallery and the physical world and limit the imagination to the constructs of the physical world. But of course, we're not really limited to that. In virtual space, we can create gigantic artworks that don't have to adhere to the laws of reality."[96]

The resulting challenge is to help artists leverage that distinction.

"Artists are trying to replicate real space in digital form, and I would like to see more outlandish virtual installations," Hansen explained. "Optimization is a huge challenge" also, he added, because "artists can make any kind of art," and the art they upload to New Art City can be formatted in "any kind of file."[97]

---

95 Ibid.
96 Ibid.
97 Ibid.

Hansen expressed hope that, ultimately, the platform will help ensure fair compensation for artists and art professionals:

"We want to create a model whereby New Art City supports and pays artists and curators fair living wages for their work. This is a huge part of this mission—and it's a hard code to crack because traditionally digital art has had a hard time gaining value, as something that can be infinitely replicated."[98]

ARTS AND TECHNOLOGY INCUBATOR

Transforming the creative economy is an issue Kaganskiy has also worked on.

In 2013, Karen Wong of the New Museum reached out to nudge Kaganskiy about a new opportunity at the intersection of arts and technology. The New Museum had plans to launch an incubator for creative professionals exploring new ideas at the intersection of art, technology, and design, and they were looking for a director to develop a vision for the new program in that space. The opportunity was right up Kaganskiy's alley—so much so she already had Google documents full of ideas she had been brainstorming for a similar concept. She used those ideas as the basis for her pitch to the New Museum, merging her vision with the museum's existing plans, and was offered the job.[99]

---

98 Ibid.
99 Kaganskiy, "The Art Incubator: Julia Kaganskiy at New Inc."

Underpinning Kaganskiy's vision for the incubator, NEW INC, was a question: "Can we create a space for this new creative class?" The incubator was designed to host a "new generation of artists, designers, filmmakers, architects, and musicians who were working across disciplines, who were experimenting with new tools, new technology," often working in a much more entrepreneurial way than were the creative professionals who had preceded them in the traditional arts industry. Kaganskiy believed that the success of artists in the digital era would hinge on their mastery of the same kind of entrepreneurial skills and innovative tools she had seen the tech sector thrive on.[100]

"When they said the word 'incubator,' I was like, 'Yeah!' That's actually exactly what the creative community needs, because we never learned these skills in art school," Kaganskiy enthused. "We never learned how to negotiate contracts or build budgets or pitch projects or work on a commercial commission from a brand, but more and more, these are how creative people are making a living today. So, if the tech industry, the food industry, or the manufacturing industry have incubator and accelerator spaces to help new start-ups get off the ground in these industries, why shouldn't the arts industry have a similar program that could lend some support and help develop these skills and strategies and new models in the creative sector? So that's ... what we set out to build."[101]

---

100 Ibid.
101 Ibid.

To illustrate the kinds of artistic tech start-ups operating in the incubator space, Kaganskiy shared the example of Print All Over Me, which she described as an "amazing platform where you can design your own fashion-and-tech-style accessories." The website has "hundreds of different items and silhouettes to choose from—everything from silk dresses to jean jumpsuits to swimsuits to backpacks"—and users can upload self-designed artwork or photographs to which they have usage rights in order to create custom-designed products they can order for their own use and make available for sale to other online shoppers.[102]

She also shared the story of Micro, a non-profit organization that builds six-foot-tall science museums designed to be featured in public spaces. These miniature museums, born at the intersection of science and design, "are designed to go in places where museums aren't," especially in what the founders call "dehumanizing zones," where people congregate but lack engagement with each other and their surroundings, such as hospital waiting rooms, airport lounges, and Department of Motor Vehicles service centers.[103]

***

As digital technologies transform the art world, physical museums, galleries, and concert halls are no longer the only access points for the fine arts. The rapid digitization of the arts has led to unprecedented access, but it has also raised questions about the role of traditional art institutions.

---

102 Ibid.
103 Ibid.

Digital strategist JiaJia Fei, the founder of the world's first digital agency for art, has devoted herself to addressing exactly these issues.

"Does the rapid digitization of images reduce the experience you have—is it reductive—or does it expand the meaning of that experience and object in an entirely new form, thereby reaching millions of people outside of the physical space who can never physically come to the museum?" Fei asked in a 2016 TEDx Talk.[104]

She went on to answer that very question: "In the history of art, the work of art is now a social object. In the future, I predict that the digitization of the work of art will completely change the physical object and dematerialize it and turn it into a social object completely defined by the conversation happening around it rather than the experience itself."[105]

In Fei's view, the transformation of artwork into a social object has two effects. First, it contributes to the digital economy, since "when a piece of content is shared online, the value of that content increases not only for the museum and the person, but the world at large." Second, it challenges traditional art institutions to become more than a physical art space by reclaiming their historical role as an "authority" on "the interpretation of art, artists, art movements, and all of the intellectual content that is surrounded by an individual work of art."[106]

---

104 JiaJia Fei, "Art in the Age of Instagram | Jia Jia Fei | TEDxMarthasVineyard," TEDx Talks, March 2, 2016, YouTube video, 13:23.
105 Ibid.
106 Ibid.

As the arts enter the digital space and are infused with technology, the arts reach a larger viewership and buyership, inspire broader conversations, remove conventional constraints on creativity, and bring into sharper relief issues and solutions regarding the fair compensation of artists.

PART II:

ARTS ADVANCE
THE SCIENCES

CHAPTER 4:

ARTISTIC PRACTICES AS SCIENTIFIC ADVANCEMENTS

Science and art sometimes can touch one another, like two pieces of the jigsaw puzzle which is our human life, and that contact may be made across the borderline between the two respective domains.

-M. C. ESCHER, GRAPHIC ARTIST (1898–1972)

When advocacy for the integration of science and the arts surfaces in public discourse, it often stresses the role of the arts in developing mind-sets that enhance technical problem-solving. According to this logic, the arts are beneficial to science insofar as they encourage creativity, out-of-the-box thinking, and human-centered design or other methodologies of innovation.

This argument has plenty of evidence to support it. Hongik University researchers Donghwy An and Dr. Nara Youn have found that openness to aesthetics and the experience of art enhances individuals' creativity by imbuing them with a sense of inspiration.[107]

However, describing art primarily as an incubator for creativity is limiting and misleading. It posits a false dichotomy between the skills and mindsets inherent to art on the one hand and science on the other. Dr. Mae Jemison—a physician, engineer, and US astronaut who was the first woman of color to travel into outer space—lamented this dichotomy in a 2002 TEDx Talk. According to popular thought, she noted, scientists are "ingenious" but "not creative," and artists are "ingenious, perhaps, but not analytical." Jemison pushed back against these rigid categorizations in her talk, advocating for a reintegration of the arts and sciences.[108]

In her talk, Jemison drew upon her own insights as both a scientist and an artist. Although she was famous for her career in science, she had also been a highly accomplished dancer in her college years who had declined the opportunity to turn professional in favor of attending medical school. When Jemison went into space, she took with her a poster of Alvin Ailey American Dance Theater's Judith Jamison performing the dance *Cry*, as well as a statue from Sierra Leone.

---

107 Donghwy An and Nara Youn, "The Inspirational Power of Art on Creativity," *Journal of Business Research* 85 (April 2018): 467–475.

108 Mae Jemison, "Mae Jemison on Teaching Arts and Sciences Together," TED, May 5, 2009, YouTube video, 16:18.

When asked why she chose to bring those items with her, she responded, "Because it represents human creativity: the creativity ... that we were required to have to conceive and build and launch the space shuttle, which springs from the same source as the imagination and analysis that it took to carve a Bundu statue, or the ingenuity it took to design, choreograph, and stage *Cry*. Each one of them are different manifestations, incarnations, of creativity—avatars of human creativity."[109]

One of the key arguments Jemison conveyed in her talk is that art does not have a monopoly on creativity. If we accept this argument as true, and if we simultaneously view art as nothing more than an incubator of creativity in service of the sciences, then, to some extent, the argument for the necessity of art is undermined. If art and science both have creativity as their wellspring, then the premise that creativity must be developed via the arts in order to be applied in the sciences might be called into question. If either the arts or the sciences could be a valid path for growing a creative mindset, then perhaps, it would follow, creativity need only be developed within the sciences.

If art only helped science do something science can already do for itself, that would imply that art is not essential to scientific advancement. However, art has much more to offer science than just the development of creative mindsets! Some incredibly inspiring and impactful scientific innovations have their origins in technical approaches taken directly from artistic practices. That is to say, the scientists who led these innovations did not create scientific achievements by

_____

109 Ibid.

dreaming up brand-new techniques; they built upon and adapted, for scientific use, pre-existing techniques artists and artisans had already invented hundreds of years earlier.

HEART-SAVING ARTISANAL WEAVING

Pediatric cardiologist Dr. Franz Freudenthal discovered the lifesaving applicability of artistic techniques to the medical field. He credits his grandmother, a physician who settled in Bolivia as a Jewish refugee, for encouraging him "to see beyond any limitation." He grew up accompanying her on medical visits as she delivered healthcare to indigenous communities in the heart of the Andes.[110]

In his own medical career, Freudenthal felt called to tackle a medical challenge that was inordinately prevalent in his home country: infant mortality. In the cloud-high altitudes of the Bolivian Altiplano, oxygen levels are very low, causing Bolivians to face twice the worldwide average risk of heart problems. Infants frequently have a congenital defect related to the lack of oxygen that causes them to be born with a hole in their heart. Solar radiation, low socioeconomic status, poor nutrition, and infections during pregnancy all further raise the risk of a Bolivian baby being born with a heart problem. The risk of losing a newborn child is so great, in fact, that parents often hesitate to name their baby until they feel reassured their child will survive. Without intervention, a mere 15 percent of affected Bolivian children survive to celebrate their fifth birthday. Yet if their heart problems are

---

110 Franz Freudenthal, "A New Way to Heal Hearts without Surgery | Franz Freudenthal," TED, September 30, 2016, YouTube video, 9:28.

detected in time, 85 percent of them live into their mid-sixties or beyond.[111]

As a medical student working in a hospital in his hometown of La Paz, Freudenthal witnessed a young child die from one such altitude-induced heart defect. He believed it was an unnecessary death, so he began working on designing lifesaving cardiac devices.[112] During a camping trip with a friend in the Amazon, inspiration struck him to create a coil-like device to close the hole in the hearts of patients with a similar cardiac anomaly. He spent thousands of hours working in a lab conducting in vitro and in vivo studies to develop a prototype for this device and received a scholarship to build upon this work through research in Germany.[113, 114]

Freudenthal and his wife, Dr. Alexandra Heath, ultimately returned to Bolivia from Germany after both completing specialized medical training there. Heath, like Freudenthal, was deeply moved by the human impact of the unusually high prevalence of cardiac anomalies in Bolivia. Thus, the two vowed to dedicate their lives not only to one another but also to the children grasping for a chance to survive and thrive.[115] They opened a center for diagnosis and treatment of congenital heart disease in La Paz, and together they resolved

111 Alexandra Heath and Franz Freudenthal, "Weaving Solutions for the Heart," La Ciudad de las Ideas, 2016, accessed August 31, 2020.

112 Alejandra Martins, "Los inventos del médico boliviano que salvó miles de niños," BBC, October 2, 2014, accessed May 15, 2021.

113 Freudenthal, "A New Way to Heal Hearts without Surgery | Franz Freudenthal."

114 Martins, "Los inventos del médico boliviano que salvó miles de niños."

115 Heath and Freudenthal, "Weaving Solutions for the Heart."

to fight side by side against death so that, one day, no family would lose a child to a congenital heart defect.

In the midst of their intense focus and purpose, they found the obstacles to improving children's heart health in Bolivia truly daunting. At the high altitudes of Bolivia, the defects were generally so large they could not be well-managed even with commercial medical devices.

Freudenthal recounted in a 2016 TEDx Talk, "With my wife and partner, Dr. Alexandra Heath, we started to see patients. After successfully treating patients with our coil, we felt really enthusiastic. But we live in a place that is twelve thousand feet high. And the patients there need a special device to solve their heart condition. The hole in altitude patients is different, because the orifice between the arteries is larger. Most patients cannot afford to be treated on time, and they die. The first coil could successfully treat only half of the patients in Bolivia."[116]

Given that the medical infrastructure was insufficient for the number of patients requiring care, open-heart surgery was unfeasible for all but the most extreme of medical cases. In the short term, Drs. Heath and Freudenthal felt so heartbroken by the loss of the children they were unable to save that they seriously considered setting aside the cause and returning to Germany.[117]

116 Freudenthal, "A New Way to Heal Hearts without Surgery | Franz Freudenthal."

117 Heath and Freudenthal, "Weaving Solutions for the Heart."

Ultimately, they held fast to their courageous intentions despite the challenges. Heath explained, "At times, we felt like running away, but we stayed in Bolivia. We rolled up our sleeves and got to work, looking for infrastructure, getting equipment, holding training sessions and conferences so that the people, our colleagues, [and] our nurses received enough training to provide care for the children."[118] As for the medical device design, Freudenthal "went back to the drawing board"—and he also started to look toward the families of his young patients as partners in problem-solving.[119]

Together, the medical team and local families arrived at a solution that had been right under their noses the whole time, albeit in a less than obvious form. Many women in the community, including mothers of babies with heart defects seeking care for their children, were highly skilled in centuries-old textile-weaving techniques. Many of the Aymara women in Bolivia had spent the better part of a lifetime perfecting their weaving skills, which they had learned as children. Freudenthal realized that the same ancestral weaving techniques in which many women in the community were expertly skilled could be readily adapted to create a device to block the hole in a patient's heart that would extend the human heart's lifespan.

Today, many Aymara artisans continue to use their weaving skills to create beautiful textiles for sale in the local marketplaces, but it is also possible to catch a glimpse of their nimble fingers working away in the medical technology industry to

---

118 Ibid.

119 Freudenthal, "A New Way to Heal Hearts without Surgery | Franz Freudenthal."

create the lifesaving Nit-Occlud device. These small, intricate devices are made of nitinol, a highly malleable nickel-titanium alloy that can be woven like thread. Although other types of cardiac occluders are machine-produced, the magic of the Nit-Occlud device is that it is made of a single nitinol filament.[120]

"There's not a single machine in the world that can make these devices with just one wire. Only these women, with their ancestral knowledge of weaving, their dedication, can make such complex structures," Freudenthal acknowledged.[121]

The devices are percutaneous, which means they are inserted through the skin, so surgery is not required. According to Freudenthal, "the device enters the body through the natural channels. Doctors have only to close the catheter through the hole. Our device expands, places itself, and closes the hole. We have this beautiful delivery system that is so simple to use because it works by itself. No open surgery [is] necessary."[122]

The devices are also highly effective. "Thanks to these devices, we can cure up to 60 percent of the diseases without opening the chest," explained Freudenthal. "The device goes through the catheters, arrives at the heart defect, recovers its shape, and in that place closes the heart defect."[123]

---

120 Ignacio de los Reyes, "The Bolivian Women Who Knit Parts for Hearts," BBC, March 29, 2015, accessed August 31, 2020.

121 "The Life-Saving Weaving of Bolivia's Indigenous Women," Great Big Story, April 25, 2017, YouTube video, 3:03.

122 Franz Freudenthal, "A New Way to Heal Hearts without Surgery | Franz Freudenthal."

123 "The Life-Saving Weaving of Bolivia's Indigenous Women."

Verónica Viro Balboa, one of the women who manufactures these devices, described the process: "The small ones take about three hours. The big ones can take a day and a half. And the weaving requires a lot of patience, affection, love of weaving." To become a Nit-Occlud manufacturer, artisanal weavers spend four months in training learning to adapt their expert artisanal skills to the purpose of creating the cardiac device, thereby putting the artistic heritage of the Aymara culture to the benefit of their community.[124]

Freudenthal has acknowledged that the impact of his work has been the product of a team effort. He told his TEDx Talk audience, "We are so proud that some of our former patients are part of our team—a team, thanks to added close interaction with patients that work with us. Together, we have only one idea: that the best solutions need to be simple." Since then, the video recording of his talk has been viewed more than 1.5 million times.[125]

In controlled medical studies, Freudenthal and Heath determined that the Nit-Occlud device was "safe and effective with very good closure rates"; they published their research in top English-language medical journals for other medical professionals to benefit from their findings.[126]

124 Ibid.
125 Freudenthal, "A New Way to Heal Hearts without Surgery | Franz Freudenthal."
126 Alexandra Heath et al., "Developing High Medical Technology, a Challenge for Developing Countries: The Percutaneous Closure of Atrial Septal Defects Using Nit-Occlud ASD-R: Early and Mid-term Results," *World Journal for Pediatric and Congenital Heart Surgery* 10 no. 4 (2019).

With these devices, more than fifty thousand patients have been successfully treated, a feat Freudenthal attributes to "the knowledge and systematization that the engineers bring, plus the ability and the art of these artists."[127]

One of those patients was Cinthia, the three-year-old daughter of Victoria Hilari. Cinthia's heart defect left her so fatigued, her mother told a BBC reporter, "she couldn't even walk one block." Three years later, her mother affirmed, "Now she can run."[128]

It is outcomes like Cinthia's that make the medical team and the artisan-engineers feel that their work is worthwhile. "We weave devices that help save lives," Viro Balboa said with a smile.[129] Her colleague, Julia Yapita Poma, feels a similar sense of fulfillment from her work.

"I learned how to weave when I was a child," said Yapita Poma. "They teach us in the schools, and our mothers tell us we must learn how to weave. I never imagined I would work like this, saving people, saving kids. For me, it is a blessing that fell upon me to work here. I feel proud."[130]

As for Freudenthal, he has said, "It seems beautiful to me that this ancestral weaving, together with this technology, is saving kids. For me, it's a miracle."[131]

127 "The Life-Saving Weaving of Bolivia's Indigenous Women."
128 de los Reyes, "The Bolivian Women Who Knit Parts for Hearts."
129 "The Life-Saving Weaving of Bolivia's Indigenous Women."
130 Ibid.
131 Ibid.

ORIGAMI-BASED ENGINEERING

Another centuries-old art form that has had a revolutionary impact on scientific engineering is the Japanese tradition of origami. Like the Bolivian weaving technique, origami involves the manipulation of a single material, which in the case of origami is a flat, square sheet of paper. A limited number of basic folds are used in combination with one another to create intricate designs ranging from the well-known paper crane to just about whatever else one might imagine.

Inside the studio of Dr. Robert J. Lang, formerly a scientist at the US National Aeronautics and Space Administration (NASA), the possibilities are on display. Across his shelves are dozens of his origami creations: a blossoming rose, a scorpion, a praying mantis, several beetles, a frog, a rhinoceros, a grasshopper, a bat, a moose, a mouse, a cat, a turtle, a sparrow, an iguana, a badger, a trout ... There are also bookcases containing rows and rows of origami books, and directly above his computer, he keeps sixteen three-ring binders labeled "Origami Designs" at hand. On his computer screen is a software script that lets him simulate the folding patterns with a graphic display, and across his desk are hand-drawn origami designs with numbered instructions on large sheets of graph paper. The drawers of his cabinets open to reveal papers of all different weights, textures, and colors. There are even more little origami creations peeking out from the nooks and crannies of his desk, and somewhere amidst the scene is the copy of his book *Origami Design Secrets: Mathematical Methods for an Ancient Art*.[132]

---

132 "See a NASA Physicist's Incredible Origami," Great Big Story, March 16, 2017, YouTube video, 3:00.

Lang has loved origami since childhood, and he brings an analytical zeal to the art form.

"Every time you crack a folding sequence or come up with a new design, you solve a problem," he said. "I think the satisfaction—the jolt of dopamine when something activates the brain's reward center—is the same thing that motivates a lot of scientists. Every time you discover something new, it's pleasurable. You want to do more of it."[133]

Lang left a career in science to pursue a full-time career as an origami artist. "I worked for NASA doing research on lasers, but throughout that whole time, I had been pursuing origami, developing designs, writing books. So, in 2001, I quit my job to try to make a career out of origami," he explained.[134]

Yet Lang does not consider origami a departure from his interest in mathematics: "I use a lot of math in my work, and that's because what's possible in origami is defined by the mathematical properties of a folded sheet of paper—so if you understand the math, you can use it to create a lot of forms that you probably wouldn't have discovered just by trial and error."[135]

He also continues to give thought to the overlaps between origami and science. "Surprisingly, origami and the structures that we've developed in origami turn out to have applications

133 Toni Feder, "Q&A: Robert Lang, Origami Master," *Physics Today*, January 8, 2018, accessed September 7, 2020.
134 "See a NASA Physicist's Incredible Origami."
135 "The Amazing Origami of Robert Lang," *Wired*, June 26, 2008, YouTube video, 2:17.

in medicine, in science, in space, in the body, consumer electronics, and more," he said in a 2008 TEDx Talk.[136]

Lang knows about these applications from personal experience.

"I've worked on a couple of different folding patterns that were round and would wrap into a cylindrical geometry to fit into a rocket, and I developed an airbag in a car that inflates from a small, folded bundle, so whenever an engineer creates something that opens and closes in a controlled way, they can make use of the folding patterns of origami," he said.[137]

***

Dr. Manan Arya has also worked on precisely this type of problem at NASA's Jet Propulsion Lab (JPL). Growing up in India, the Delhi-born engineer thought "astronauts were the coolest people ever" and wanted to be one—until he considered that, under pressure, he might "push all the wrong buttons" on the spacecraft. Instead, he channeled his enthusiasm about aeronautics into a related career. "If you can't fly a spacecraft, the next best thing is to build a spacecraft instead," Arya said—and that is how he ended up using the mathematical principles of origami to design expandable structures that can be neatly crunched into small spaces.[138]

---

136 Robert Lang, "The Math and Magic of Origami | Robert Lang," TED, July 31, 2008, YouTube video, 18:03.
137 "See a NASA Physicist's Incredible Origami."
138 "Caltech Alumnus Manan Arya: Origami ... in Space!" caltech, April 26, 2017, YouTube video, 3:39.

"In space, bigger is better," Arya said, smiling, explaining that greater surface area equals "more thrust" and "more power" for the structures that are launched into space. Yet to get into outer space, they need to start out much smaller. "I call it the suitcase problem," Arya remarked, likening the challenge of packaging large structures into a rocket to trying to "fill as much of your suitcase as possible with clothing."[139]

A challenge astronomers face in increasing understanding of the physical universe is imaging planets outside our solar system that are overshadowed by the brighter stars they orbit. Astronomers have detected these exoplanets via indirect means for over fifteen years, but actually taking a picture of them requires blocking out the extraneous light.[140] (Think about it like the problem of taking a picture of someone when the sun is shining directly behind them.)[141]

"One of the ways in which we're thinking about suppressing the starlight is using something called Starshade, which is a very large external occulter that flies in front of a space telescope and blocks out that starlight so we can image that really faint planet right next to it," explained Arya.[142]

To put the challenges in perspective, a star can be billions of times brighter than the planet that orbits it. As for the

139 Ibid.
140 Joshua Rodriguez, "Flower Power: NASA Reveals Spring Starshade Animation," National Aeronautics and Space Administration, accessed September 1, 2020.
141 "How NASA Engineers Use Origami to Design Future Spacecraft," Seeker, March 25, 2018, YouTube video, 4:20.
142 Ibid.

Starshade, just how large is "very large"? The structure is roughly the size of a professional baseball field.

"Because the biggest rockets we have right now are only about five meters in diameter, we have to come up with a way of folding up this very large structure … so that we can launch it inside a rocket, and once it gets to space, it can unfold itself. And origami is one mechanism by which we can do that, because it gives us the underlying mathematics of how large, thin sheets fold up," Arya elaborated.[143]

***

Across the country, in the labs of the University of Massachusetts Lowell, origami is proving its potential for the biomedical applications to which Lang alluded. Dr. Gulden Camci-Unal, an assistant professor of chemical engineering, and her team of student researchers are using origami-inspired structures to address the shortage of body tissues available for patients who need transplants. Cells can be grown in a lab, but the challenge is getting them to stick together in the right three-dimensional structure.

To meet this challenge, Camci-Unal's team has experimented with different natural and synthetic materials to create scaffolds (tissues templates that promote the growth of bone cells and help them harden faster). One of the materials they have used is plain paper, which Camci-Unal described as "a low-cost, widely available, and extremely flexible material that

---

143 Ibid.

can be easily fabricated into 3D structures of various shapes, sizes, and configurations."[144]

Thanks to her research, these paper scaffolds could someday be used to repair, replace, or regenerate essential parts of the human body. By using a material from everyday life, this "simple, accessible, and inexpensive" approach to tissue engineering will have the potential to help patients across the globe, even in countries with limited equipment and resources.[145]

***

All of these examples carry the echoes of the message Lang has been sharing for a decade or more: artistic techniques can be adopted to create valuable scientific and technological impact.

"When you get math involved, problems that you solve for aesthetic value only, or to create something beautiful, turn around and turn out to have an application in the real world. And as weird and surprising as it may sound, origami may someday even save a life," Lang told his TEDx Talk audience.[146]

---

144 Edwin L. Aguirre, "Finding Inspiration in Origami and Eggshells," University of Massachusetts Lowell, October 15, 2019, accessed September 7, 2020.

145 Gulden Camci-Unal and Michelle A. Nguyen, "Reimagining Eggshells and Other Everyday Items to Grow Human Tissues and Organs," The Conversation, September 18, 2019, accessed August 24, 2020.

146 Lang, "The Math and Magic of Origami | Robert Lang."

CHAPTER 5:

ART AIDS SCIENTIFIC THINKING

———

Both science and art have to do with ordered complexity.

-LANCELOT LAW WHYTE, PHILOSOPHER

AND THEORETICAL PHYSICIST (1896–1972)

The arts can greatly aid scientists, technologists, engineers, and mathematicians in sharing their knowledge with non-specialist and general audiences. The arts make it possible to illustrate, simulate, and communicate complex structural and spatial data and dynamic, intricate processes. In that way, the arts go one step further: they even help the scientists themselves think through the answers to difficult research questions and, ultimately, make scientific discoveries.

"Is there really a difference between ... a mind contemplating the relationship of light and mass ... and a mind contemplating the relationship of light ... and shadow?" asked American jazz musician and physiologist Dr. Warren Karp in a TEDx Talk he gave in March 2016.[147]

Multiple scientists have expressed a belief that artistic and scientific thinking are intertwined. Dr. Manan Arya said of his origami-inspired work as an engineer at NASA's Jet Propulsion Lab (JPL), "I don't use separate parts of my mind when I'm doing art versus when I'm doing engineering. They both involve creating things that have not yet existed." Indeed, origami helps him to think through large-scale engineering projects: "I can fold simple models at a small scale and immediately see, 'Is it going to work?'"[148]

Similarly, Dr. Makola Abdullah, the president of Virginia State University, said in a May 2016 TEDx Talk, "To me, it's all the same. It's one mind. It's not a 'left brain' or a 'right brain'—and that theory has been debunked anyway—but it's the whole brain. It's the whole mind! And when you can have those things bleeding from one side into the other, you've got something." As examples, Abdullah pointed to Leonardo da Vinci, known for his artistic masterpieces as well as his sketches of "early helicopters and early airplanes," and his own "greatest inspiration," ancient Egyptian physician, architect, poet, and sculptor Imhotep.[149]

As for Karp, he has dreamed of a world in which "scientists seek to understand complex data on an artistic level,

---

147 Warren Karp, "'Art and Science' OR 'Art or Science'? | Warren Karp | TEDxAugusta," TEDx Talks, March 7, 2016, YouTube video, 12:50.

148 "Caltech Alumnus Manan Arya: Origami ... in Space!"

149 Makola Abdullah, "STEM and the Arts | Dr. Makola Abdullah | TEDxRVA," TEDx Talks, May 26, 2016, YouTube video, 10:00.

a perceptual level." In his TEDx Talk, Karp told his audience, "I'm talking about understanding data by looking at it, walking through it, touching it, smelling it, feeling it—an immersive 3D virtual world of scientific data experienced as art. It may be the only way to even approach understanding the complexity of the universe."[150]

SCIENTIFIC MODELING THROUGH DANCE

For molecular biologist and science journalist Dr. John Bohannon, the usefulness of dance to researchers in their processes of scientific inquiry was "the most surprising thing" he discovered while running the annual Dance Your PhD contest, which *Science* magazine and the American Association for the Advancement of Science (AAAS) have held for over a decade to challenge scientists around the world to explain their research through interpretive dance. In a 2011 TEDx Talk, Bohannon shared his amazement that "some scientists are now working directly with dancers on their research," giving the example of biomedical engineer Dr. David Odde at the University of Minnesota, who "works with dancers to study how cells move." On stage, Bohannon proceeded to elaborate on how cells move by changing their shape, as artists from the Black Label Movement dance troupe illustrated the slow, oozing movement on the outside and the chaotic explosions and reattachments on the inside. "Now, David builds mathematical models of this and then he tests those in the lab," continued Bohannon, "but before he

---

150 Karp, "'Art and Science' OR 'Art or Science'? | Warren Karp | TEDxAugusta."

does that, he works with dancers to figure out what kinds of models to build in the first place."[151]

At Princeton University, an entire experimental laboratory emerged to research flocking behavior through dance. In 2009, Dr. Naomi Leonard, a professor of mechanical and aerospace engineering who researches the collective motion of schools of fish and flocks of birds, met her Princeton colleague Susan Marshall after giving a public lecture on her work. Listening to Leonard's presentation on flocking behavior, Marshall, a choreographer, wondered what would happen if she asked dancers to apply the same rules of movement fish or birds use. She suggested to Leonard that they collaborate on a project. Coincidentally, Leonard also happened to be a dancer, and she seized the opportunity to bridge her scientific and artistic interests.[152]

About a year later, the pair teamed up with members of Marshall's professional dance troupe, dancer and non-dancer students, and community members to create an art and engineering project exploring how the feedback laws used to model flocking translate when applied by dancers. They ended up transforming the project, called "Flock Logic," into a semester-long course open to students from all schools.

The primary finding that arose from their analyses of the filmed performances is that "some leaders seemed to spontaneously emerge in the troupe in mid-motion," according

151 John Bohannon, "Dance vs. PowerPoint, a Modest Proposal—John Bohannon," TED-Ed, November 28, 2012, YouTube video, 11:17.

152 Cassandra Willyard, "The Agony and Ecstasy of Cross-disciplinary Collaboration," *Science*, August 27, 2013, accessed August 29, 2020.

to a *Science* article featuring the collaboration. The scientific insights revealed in the "Flock Logic" project were ultimately published as a book chapter in an anthology of technical research, *Controls and Art: Inquiries at the Intersection of the Subjective and the Objective*, and incorporated into a downloadable flock simulator.[153, 154]

IMPROVISATIONAL ACTING FOR ENGINEERS

At Northwestern University, Dr. Joseph Holtgrieve, the assistant dean for undergraduate engineering, has leveraged the power of another performing art to improve scientific thinking. Holtgrieve has taught improvisational acting for over twenty-five years as a method for "helping struggling engineering students think and act productively when facing moments of intense uncertainty." He sees improv, "an art form designed to help a person focus on the needs of others," as a valuable means of helping his students learn to turn obstacles into opportunities.[155]

"If you're unfamiliar with the principles of improv, they include 'Just say yes,' 'Start anywhere,' and 'Embrace your mistakes,'" explained Holtgrieve in an *Inside Higher Ed* article about his course. "As it happens, these are also essential skills for the effective problem-solving and design innovation that is central to the study of engineering."[156]

---

153 Naomi E. Leonard et al., "In the Dance Studio: An Art and Engineering Exploration of Human Flocking," Princeton University, accessed September 29, 2020.

154 "Flock Logic," Princeton University, accessed September 29, 2020.

155 Joseph Holtgrieve, "The Lessons of Engineering Improv," *Inside Higher Ed*, January 11, 2018, accessed August 29, 2020.

156 Ibid.

Holtgrieve elaborated by drawing an analogy between group scene exercises in improvisational acting and real-life projects in engineering:

"[In improv,] participants commit to a character and to a common set of assumptions and boundaries before committing to each other as they enter a scene. Agreeing on the context of the scene allows the players the freedom to let the content emerge through connection, which is the true joy of improv and an extraordinary thing to witness. The same thing happens in engineering, but the context is the problem, the commitment is to the team and the process of user-centered problem-solving, and the content that's allowed to emerge consists of the users' underlying needs and interests—which leads to a user-centered solution."[157]

Across the country, other leading universities have started to offer theater classes and workshops to help science and engineering students hone their communication skills.

Dr. Ed Scheinerman, a professor of applied mathematics and statistics and the vice dean for graduate education at Johns Hopkins University's Whiting School of Engineering, launched an improv class for STEM students in 2017, as part of an effort to help them translate their findings to colleagues and non-scientists. In Scheinerman's view, improvisational acting boosts students' "self-confidence and communication skills" and helps them develop the skills necessary to

---

157 Ibid.

listen to and influence decision-makers in "high-pressure situations."[158]

However, Holtgrieve and other leaders in higher education also see improvisational acting as offering cognitive benefits in relation to teamwork.

"It's a way to practice certain cognitive functions that help you communicate," explained Dr. Stephanie Pulford, then the associate director of instructional research and development at the University of California, Davis's Center for Educational Effectiveness. "You have to affirm what the person who spoke before you said and move forward, and that's a skill we rarely scaffold."[159]

Aditya Jain, who took improvisation at Northwestern University while studying industrial engineering and applied mathematics, found this skill essential to the tasks of an engineer.

"'Say yes' is incredibly important when it comes to brainstorming," Jain said. "'Just show up,' 'start anywhere,' and 'act now' are very relevant to the iterative design process where a person or team needs to be ready to continuously push out ideas and try different things."[160]

Jacob Hullings, who also studied improvisation along with engineering at Northwestern, noted that the cognitive

---

158 Margaret Loftus, "Command Performance," *Prism*, May 2018, accessed March 9, 2021.

159 Ibid.

160 Amanda Morris, "Engineers Learn the Art of Allowing," Northwestern University, May 26, 2016, accessed March 9, 2021.

flexibility he developed in improv class transferred to project-based work in other courses.[161]

"Whenever you are solving a problem in engineering, there's a lot that can change without notice, and you have to be ready to adapt to that," Hullings said.[162]

To boost such flexibility, Holtgrieve's co-instructor, Byron Stewart, has designed the courses to minimize preparation and maximize mindfulness.

"Of course, you need to prepare in certain situations, but it's the whole idea of flexibility that crosses over [into engineering], being comfortable with your plan not working," Stewart explained.[163]

SOLVING SCIENTIFIC PROBLEMS WITH MUSIC

For Dr. Makola Abdullah, music is the art form that has given him his eureka moments. Abdullah explained in a TEDx Talk in May 2016 how his love of jazz informed his thought process as he was conducting doctoral research in engineering:

"When I was working on my dissertation, which was reducing the vibrations of tall buildings during earthquakes, I would imagine the buildings as men or women that were dancing out of control to seismic music. And then from that analogy, how do I prevent that? How can we turn down the music?

---

161 Loftus, "Command Performance."
162 Ibid.
163 Ibid.

How do we isolate the music so that the dancer doesn't have to dance as much? Or can I change the rhythm of the music so that the dancer can't hear and won't dance the same way?"[164]

After completing his dissertation, Abdullah went on to author dozens of published academic papers on earthquake and wind engineering and to open the US Government–funded Center of Excellence at Virginia State University, a key goal of which is "increasing diversity in the science, technology, engineering, agriculture, and mathematics (STEAM) pipeline."[165]

***

More recently, music has been harnessed in the search for a way to counter COVID-19.

In early April 2020, while I was under stay-at-home orders because of the pandemic, a *Science* article headline caught my eye: "Scientists Have Turned the Structure of the Coronavirus into Music." This I have to hear, I thought.

I wondered whether the coronavirus's tune would be catchier than the title of the SoundCloud file, "Viral Counterpoint of the Coronavirus Spike Protein (2019-nCoV)." I suspected not.

The first few string-plucks of the koto—a Japanese instrument the researchers chose for the musical representation—filled

---

164 Abdullah, "STEM and the Arts | Dr. Makola Abdullah | TEDxRVA."
165 "USDA Invests $4.8 Million in Three 1890 Centers of Excellence," US Department of Agriculture, June 3, 2020, accessed March 8, 2021.

my ears. After hearing just three chords, I groaned, "Oh no, this is going to be as atonal as Arnold Schoenberg's 'Pierrot lunaire.'" (If you have never listened to music that has no tonal center and are not sure what emotions are typically associated with it, angst, hysteria, and *Weltschmerz* are a few words that come to mind.)

Yet as I continued to listen to the coronavirus spike protein music—and a synthesized flute-like instrument entered with a slow crescendo—the music seemed to turn into some kind of highly developed polyphony. To my surprise, the music became … not unpleasant. If I were stranded on a desert island with very limited music options, I would prefer "Viral Counterpoint of the Coronavirus Spike Protein (2019-nCoV)" to "Pierrot lunaire" any day.

As I scrolled back up to the audio file description, I found that the scientist behind the sonification of the coronavirus's structure—Dr. Markus J. Buehler, department head and professor of civil and environmental engineering at the Massachusetts Institute of Technology (MIT)—had explicitly discussed the virus's "musical deceit."

"As you listen to the protein, you will find that the intricate design results in incredibly interesting and actually pleasing, relaxing sounds. This doesn't really convey the deadly impacts this particular protein is having on the world. This aspect of the music shows the deceiving nature of the virus, how it hijacks our body to replicate, and hurt us along the way. So, the music is a metaphor for this nature of the virus to deceive the host and exploit it for its own multiplication," Buehler wrote.[166]

Why set a virus to music at all, though? As Buehler argued, "The new format can help scientists find sites on the protein where antibodies or drugs might be able to bind—simply by searching for specific musical sequences that correspond to these sites."[167]

The dynamic structure of the COVID-19 pathogen is what lends it to being represented in the form of music, and why it is helpful to represent it in that way. "Molecules aren't static as [is] assumed in textbooks. They are actually continuously moving, vibrating, and we discovered that they generate a sort of molecular sound due to their quantum-level motions," Buehler explained.[168]

Buehler and his team's research is designed to fill gaps in knowledge about the formation, structure, and function of the proteins of the COVID-19 pathogen. Each of the amino acids, or "chemical 'Lego bricks,'" of the DNA has a "unique vibrational signature," and by turning that vibration into sound, the proteins become audible.[169]

For Buehler, this musical approach to virology is first and foremost aimed at "trying to better understand the COVID-19

166 Vineeth Venugopal, "Scientists Have Turned the Structure of the Coronavirus into Music," *Science*, April 3, 2020, accessed August 24, 2020.

167 Ibid.

168 Markus J. Buehler, "If A Virus Could Sing," Falling Walls, accessed November 21, 2020.

169 Ibid.

pathogen and help to develop treatments," but it is also about "getting more people excited about the interface of art and science—and music in particular as a universal language that connects people across the world."[170]

Buehler's research has revealed that vibrations of the protein spikes on coronaviruses, including the one that causes COVID-19, play a crucial part in allowing the virus to penetrate human cells. In October 2020, he co-authored an article on the role the vibrations of coronavirus proteins may play in infection.[171] Buehler and his colleague Yiwen Hu found "a strong direct relationship between the rate and intensity of the spikes' vibrations and how readily the virus could penetrate the cell," and "an opposite relationship with the fatality rate of a given coronavirus," according to an article in *MIT News*. This vibration-based method of understanding "the detailed molecular structure of these proteins" could therefore be used to "screen emerging coronaviruses or new mutations of COVID-19" to "quickly assess their potential risk."[172]

170 Markus Buehler, "Breaking the Wall of Matter and Sound: If a Virus Could Sing," Falling Walls, accessed January 22, 2021.

171 Yiwen Hu and Markus J. Buehler, "Comparative Analysis of Nanomechanical Features of Coronavirus Spike Proteins and Correlation with Lethality and Infection Rate," *Matter* 4 (January 6, 2021): 1–11.

172 David L. Chandler, "Vibrations of Coronavirus Proteins May Play a Role in Infection," Massachusetts Institute of Technology (MIT), November 19, 2020, accessed November 21, 2020.

***

The power to facilitate thinking about complex scientific and mathematical concepts is one of the greatest advantages the arts have to offer.

CHAPTER 6:

ART AS STEM EDUCATION AND SCIENCE COMMUNICATION

———

Science provides an understanding of a universal experience. Arts provide a universal understanding of a personal experience.

-MAE JEMISON, ENGINEER, PHYSICIAN, AND ASTRONAUT (1956–PRESENT)

Where the universal understanding that science provides meets the personal understanding that the arts provide is where powerful storytelling takes place—the kind of storytelling that can educate, edify, and inspire. Whether it is to teach students, share research findings, or enlighten the public, art can serve as an apt medium for communicating scientific knowledge.

SCIENCE COMEDY

Science writer Kasha Patel brings her passion for science communication to the world of the performing arts as a comedian.

When Kasha Patel first broke into comedy as a graduate student in science journalism, she tried making jokes about science. "That's what I was going to school for, and that's what I was surrounded by," she said.[173]

The science jokes mostly fell flat, though. "It wasn't really working, because I wasn't very good at comedy," Patel admitted. As a newcomer to stand-up performance, she was still learning the basics: how to "hold a microphone" and "not be awkward on stage." The world of comedy, especially in Boston, was "very much a boys' club," and Patel stuck out. "I'm a nerd!" Patel laughed, recounting that getting her foot into comedy was like "breaking into someone's club."[174]

Not wanting to lose her audience, she switched to making jokes about herself and her upbringing as an Indian American in West Virginia. It was not until she came to Washington, DC, to work for NASA that she began performing science-themed comedy.[175]

When her colleagues at NASA found out she did stand-up comedy, they asked, "Oh, do you do jokes about science?" Patel replied, "Oh, you would come to a show about science?"

---

173 Kasha Patel, virtual Creator Speaker Series with Eric Koester hosted by the Creator Institution, October 14, 2020.

174 Ibid.

175 Ibid.

They said yes, and the rest is history. "The demand required that I write science jokes," Patel concluded.[176]

Although Patel has found a particular niche producing one of the only science comedy shows in the United States, she prides herself on creating high-quality comedy that has value outside of that niche. "When I go into my science comedy show that I produce, I try and compare it to regular stand-up comedy, not necessarily like 'A proton walks into a bar' kind of science comedy."[177]

In doing this work, her long-term goal is to "make science more mainstream for the general public." In her ideal world, mainstream entertainment would include "funny science comedy that's informative," and not just "silly"—and she is paving the way for that to happen.[178]

ILLUSTRATING SCIENTIFIC DISCOVERY
For hundreds of years, art has been used to capture and convey specialized scientific knowledge. Quintessential Renaissance man Leonardo da Vinci filled countless notebooks with anatomical sketches, which not only revolutionized artistic depiction of the human form but also advanced scientific understanding of the human body. Albrecht Dürer, a great artist of the Northern Renaissance, also greatly influenced sixteenth-century science with his cartographic and anatomical work, from a map of brain function to star charts of

---

176 Ibid.
177 Ibid.
178 Ibid.

the northern and southern hemispheres. The collection of French-American naturalist John James Audubon's nineteenth-century watercolor prints of North American birds, *Birds of America,* is one of the finest ornithological works to date.

To this day, art remains a useful means of communicating scientific knowledge. Much of what started with da Vinci, who is considered the father of medical illustration, continues today as professionally trained artists collaborate with scientists and physicians to render complex life science information into visual depictions.

"Medical and scientific illustration takes the overwhelming natural world and puts it into manageable chunks so you can understand the concepts without reading pages and pages of text," medical and scientific illustrator Ikumi Kayama explained in a TEDx Talk in Washington, DC.[179]

Furthermore, scientific illustrators "can bring [out] the important details" in their art, or depict an object as "see-through" in order to reveal underlying structures, creating a 3D-like effect, Kayama explained. Every time a new medical procedure is developed or a new scientific discovery needs to be communicated to the public, she added, a medical illustration is created. "So as long as there [are] advancements in science, there is going to be a need to create illustrations to make the discoveries relevant and accessible to everyone."[180]

---

179 Ikumi Kayama, "The Art of Science and the Science of Art | Ikumi Kayama | TEDxFoggyBottom," TEDx Talks, May 6, 2015, YouTube video, 6:01.
180 Ibid.

Kayama's suggestion that visual renderings make scientific understanding more "manageable" is supported by a body of research. Humans are visual thinkers, and when presented with complex concepts, it is our instinct to model those concepts visually in our minds. A study conducted by researchers at Brown University, Massachusetts General Hospital, the Massachusetts Institute of Technology, and Harvard Medical School found that even when people are prompted to use verbal thinking, they create visual images to accompany their inner speech, suggesting that visual thinking is deeply ingrained in the brain.[181] Drs. Eliza Bobek and Barbara Tversky found that when students created their own visualizations of scientific concepts, they learned better.[182]

Many topics in science are notoriously difficult to learn because they involve dynamic mechanisms, processes, and behaviors of complex systems. As Bobek and Tversky acknowledged, "Learners must master not only the individual components of the system or process (structure) but also the interactions and mechanisms (function)."[183] For example, studying anatomy and physiology is not just a matter of learning the sizes and shapes of organs and where they are situated in the body. It also involves learning how those bodily structures interact with one another to sustain the body as a whole.

---

181 Elinor Amit et al., "An Asymmetrical Relationship between Verbal and Visual Thinking: Converging Evidence from Behavior and fMRI," *NeuroImage* 152 (2017): 619–627.
182 Eliza Bobek and Barbara Tversky, "Creating Visual Explanations Improves Learning," *Cognitive Research: Principles and Implications* 1 no. 1 (2016): 27.
183 Ibid.

However, pictures are two-dimensional and static, while scientific processes involve many intricate moving parts. What if we considered that there is a higher-dimensional, dynamic art form that, like scientific processes, involves individual components of a system and the interactions between them?

DANCING COMPLEX CONCEPTS

That art form is dance—and even I, as a dancer, was surprised to discover how long and how frequently people have been using it to embody and illustrate complex scientific concepts. When I first learned of the Dance Your PhD contest from integrative medicine researcher and engineer Dr. Perry Skeath, I was intrigued.

Curious to determine whether such an initiative arose out of thin air or whether there were similar precedents, I was amazed to discover that scientists had staged a "chemical ballet" as early as 1939 at an American Chemical Society meeting in Baltimore.[184] It amazed me to think that, less than a quarter-century after the premiere of a modernist ballet scandalized its audience in Paris to the point that—legend has it—riots broke out, chemists were prancing about as "hydrogen atoms" and "carbon atoms" in a ballet demonstrating the synthesis of radioactive benzene from acetylene.[185]

---

184 "Scientific Movement: The Art of Science and Dance," The Science & Entertainment Exchange, accessed September 29, 2020.
185 Ibid.

In the decades to follow, scientists were not just dancing technical concepts; they were also capturing that dance on film. In 1971, two hundred young Californians gathered in a sports field at Stanford University to simulate the molecular dynamics of protein synthesis with their own bodies. The thirteen-minute film, entitled *Protein Synthesis: An Epic on the Cellular Level*, was the brainchild of a couple of medical students who had approached Dr. Paul Berg, then the chairman of Stanford's Department of Biochemistry, for technical advice and funding. Professor Berg gave them the green light, and the students assembled a film crew and a cadre of dancers and shot the film in a single day.[186]

Gabriel Weiss, who directed the film, eventually became a doctor of internal medicine and led a twenty-piece jazz band, and Kent Wilson, who produced it, went on to become a professor of chemistry at the University of California, San Diego. The dance itself was choreographed by Jackie Benington, who later married Weiss. As for Professor Berg, he got a starring role in the film introducing the leading players: 30S Ribosome, mRNA, and Initiator Factor One.[187]

Jackie Benington Weiss reflected decades later that the *Protein Synthesis* dance had "manifested from cultural loosening," emerging to challenge "rigidity in science education"

186 Lauren Young, "In 1971, Stanford Students Did an Interpretive Dance to Demonstrate Protein Synthesis," Atlas Obscura, March 10, 2017, accessed August 29, 2020.

187 Gabriel Weiss, "Protein Synthesis: An Epic on the Cellular Level," Internet Archive, November 29, 2013, accessed August 29, 2020.

in the same way that their artistic contemporaries had challenged "the rigid confines of dance practices."[188] Loosening the rigidity of science education apparently held appeal for science instructors and students alike. Celebrated within scientific circles, *Protein Synthesis* became a landmark dance that has been viewed in chemistry classes for almost fifty years.[189]

***

Around the time the *Protein Synthesis* dancers were rolling around on the green, Dr. James ("Jim") Simons was chairing the mathematics department at Stony Brook University. A mathematician with a PhD from the University of California, Berkeley who returned to academia after working as a codebreaker during the Vietnam War, Simons went on to become a hedge fund manager and philanthropist.

When it came to funding STEM education, Simons did not stop at the obvious. Several years after founding the non-profit organization Math for America, Dr. Simons commissioned a dance project inspired by differential cohomology, a mathematical theory he had developed in his doctoral dissertation.

What, then, is differential cohomology? Dr. Andrew Jay Stimpson, on whose doctoral dissertation committee Simons served, explains it in the opening line of his dissertation: "A

188 Jackie Benington Weiss, "Protein Synthesis: An Epic on the Cellular Level," *MATTERS OF ACT: A Journal of Ideas* 1 (Winter 2017): 52–53.

189 Sanjoy Roy, "Dance+: Protein Synthesis—an Epic on the Cellular Level," *Springback Magazine*, August 11, 2020, accessed September 26, 2020.

differential cohomology theory is a type of extension of a cohomology theory E^* restricted to smooth manifolds that encodes information that is not homotopy invariant."[190]

Gulp. That is a lot of highly specialized terminology!

In *The Making of Differential Cohomology*, a behind-the-scenes documentary about the dance, Simons described differential cohomology as "a somewhat new way of looking at certain aspects of geometry" that is "very abstract and involves calculus."

(Alternatively, an *Institutional Investor* article explained that "differential geometry, Simons's specialty, is the study of curved surfaces and spaces.")[191]

Fortunately, New York City–based dancer and choreographer Kyla Barkin did not skip a beat when Simons explained his mathematical theory to her during a walk together one autumn morning in New York's Central Park.

"When we were walking together, he was discussing the talk that he would be giving on the subject of differential cohomology, and he began to explain the subject itself and then said, 'That sounds like a great title for a dance,' and I said

---

190 Andrew Jay Stimpson, "Axioms for Differential Cohomology" (PhD diss., Stony Brook University, 2011).

191 Hal Lux, "The Secret World of Jim Simons," *Institutional Investor Magazine*, November 1, 2000, accessed September 29, 2020.

'Well, it sounds like a great dance, period,'" Barkin recounted in the documentary.[192]

Simons then commissioned dancers to demonstrate the theory he had developed at the opening of the Simons Center for Geometry and Physics International Workshop on Differential Cohomology at Stony Brook University.[193] Thus, in January 2011, the Barkin/Selissen project presented the world premiere of the modern dance piece *Differential Cohomology*.[194]

To prepare the piece, Barkin and her co-choreographer, Aaron Selissen, worked with Simons to bridge the realms of dance and mathematics.

The dance was based on a diagram of a hexagon with particular topographic qualities, and the dancers used the movement of their bodies to physically represent different algebraic objects within that diagram.

"As far as how the piece developed, Jim had defined [eight] terms for us to be able to understand the diagram and theory," Barkin explained. "I took those [eight] terms and created one movement for each, then either accumulated or subtracted

192 "Differential Cohomology Documentary," Barkin/Selissen Project, June 13, 2017, YouTube video, 15:00.
193 "Kyla Barkin and Aaron Selissen Present World Premiere of Differential Cohomology, New Dance Work Inspired by Mathematical Theory," *The Dance Enthusiast*, 2011, accessed September 29, 2020.
194 "Getting to Know Kyla Barkin," *Monkeyhouse*, January 17, 2014, accessed September 29, 2020.

to create two phrases. When executed simultaneously, there would be some perfect unison and some variation."[195]

However, the choreographers took some artistic license in order to adapt the representation of the theory into a compelling dance performance. For example, if the dancers representing the moving parts along the six points of the diagram had followed the theory strictly, they would only have been able to move from stage right to stage left.[196]

"Jim recognized this as an issue for [the] stage," Barkin said. Just as the dancers brought an openness to learning new concepts to the challenge of incorporating mathematics into their art, Simons brought an appreciation and understanding of aesthetic considerations to the shared endeavor.[197]

"It didn't give a great deal of insight into the geometry, but at least it showed there was a pattern of mappings, and it was that pattern of mappings that I thought might make a good dance," Simons said of the resulting piece.[198]

For the dancers themselves, the fusion of their art form with mathematical concepts was quite a novelty.

"When I found out that the principal theme of the project was based on a mathematical theory, I was definitely interested,"

195 "Kyla Barkin and Aaron Selissen Present World Premiere of Differential Cohomology, New Dance Work Inspired by Mathematical Theory."
196 Ibid.
197 Ibid.
198 "Differential Cohomology Documentary," Barkin/Selissen Project, June 13, 2017, YouTube video, 15:00.

recounted one dancer, who noted that dance "is usually from more of a visceral and human place" and recalled his curiosity to see how that aspect would be combined with "something that was a bit more calculated and scientific."[199]

"I was interested to see how the [set of] rules of the math that they were dealing with was going to dictate how we were going to make the movement and how it would inform what we were doing," the dancer added.[200]

Yet the dancers were not simply given directed movements to perform; the more they danced, the more they internalized these mathematical rules and learned to work within them creatively. (They also received several hours of mathematics lectures!)[201]

The dancers first "started playing with angles and lines," and as they "became more familiar with the concept, then we started pulling from that and shaping that movement, and transitioning between fluid and linear movement, or transitioning between heavy and light movement," said Selissen.[202]

The Barkin/Selissen Project performed *Differential Cohomology* at the internationally acclaimed Jacob's Pillow Dance Festival in 2012.[203] In 2019, the Barkin/Selissen Project brought the hour-long performance—redubbed *Dance of*

---

199 Ibid.
200 Ibid.
201 Ibid.
202 Ibid.
203 "Jacob's Pillow Dance 2012," Berkshire Fine Arts, June 7, 2012, accessed November 21, 2020.

the Diagram—to the National Math Festival in Washington, DC, which is how I first heard of it.[204]

***

Science-related dance continues to have a place in academia through the Dance Your PhD contest. "Most people would not normally think of interpretive dance as a tool for scientific communication," Alexa Meade, one of the judges of the contest, said in an interview with *Science* magazine. "However, the body can express conceptual thoughts through movement in ways that words and data tables cannot. The results are both artfully poetic and scientifically profound."[205]

The winner of the 2018 contest was Pramodh Senarath Yapa, a physicist at the University of Alberta. "Superconductivity relies on lone electrons pairing up when cooled below a certain temperature," Yapa said. "Once I began to think of electrons as unsociable people who suddenly become joyful once paired up, imagining them as dancers was a no-brainer!" After six weeks of choreographing and songwriting about superconductivity, Yapa had an entertaining, thoroughly nerdy music video that won him top marks from the contest judges.[206]

---

204 "Dance of the Diagram," National Math Festival, accessed November 21, 2020.

205 John Bohannon, "The Winner of This Year's 'Dance Your Ph.D.' Contest Turned Physics into Art," *Science*, February 15, 2019, accessed August 29, 2020.

206 Ibid.

"Using sweet partner dancing for the Cooper Pairs of shy electrons and aggressive metalheads as the spin impurities, Pramodh was able to create an intuitive visual representation for the nonlocal electrodynamics of superconductivity," Meade said.[207]

IMPROVING SCIENCE COMMUNICATION THROUGH IMPROV

In addition to being used as a vehicle for science communication, the performing arts are used as exercises to improve the skills behind effective science communication. One researcher at the forefront of this effort, on both the practical and theoretical levels, is Nichole Bennett.

As a graduate research fellow at the National Science Foundation, Nichole Bennett was confident she could help tackle one of the greatest challenges of our time. Bennett studied a particular species of butterfly to further understanding of climate change. Her attitude, as she later recounted with a laugh, was "I'm gonna solve this!"[208]

What Bennett was not so confident about was whether people outside of her field would understand her research and why it mattered. She realized there was "a bigger problem than just the butterflies." She thought to herself, *Oh, people are having trouble understanding what I'm saying as a scientist.* Bennett was not the only one with a science communication problem. She was seeing other scientists "have a lot of trouble getting

---

207 Ibid.
208 Nichole Bennett, "STEMprov on Austin Public," Nichole Bennett, July 19, 2018, YouTube video, 7:47.

across why their research is important and why we should care." She also noticed the public was "feeling disgruntled, like they don't feel like a part of science and they feel like scientists don't have much heart."[209]

After completing her master's degree in ecology and evolutionary biology at the University of Texas at Austin, Bennett found a job in the technology sector. In her free time, she became involved in improvisational theater. While doing improv acting, she had the thought, *Oh, I bet a lot of these tools from the arts could help scientists.* Thus was born her science communication workshop, STEMprov. Bennett had doubts about teaching improv to STEM specialists. She worried, *I don't even know if this is a thing that people are going to want.* Yet she figured that if there was a chance it could help them improve their science communication skills, hosting the workshop was worth a try.[210]

Bennett's hypothesis was that introducing scientists to the techniques of improvisational acting would inspire them to approach science communication as a collaborative conversation rather than a one-sided lecture.

"I think a lot of scientists … come from academic backgrounds, so their only model is … this professor at the head of a classroom, like, 'I'm the expert and I have all the knowledge, and if I just *spray* knowledge at you in the best

209 Ibid.
210 Ibid.

way, you'll get it!'" Bennett explained with a wry expression, adding, "It's ineffective."[211]

What happens if we approach it more like improv? Bennett wondered.[212]

Bennett had plenty of her own experience experimenting with different approaches to science communication. For over five years, she had hosted a weekly radio talk show called *They Blinded Me with Science*, for which she interviewed guest researchers and presented science news on UT Austin's student radio station, KVRX 91.7 FM. She had seized many opportunities to share her own research with the general public through scientific outreach initiatives in non-traditional venues, from concert halls to middle school classrooms to pubs. She had also trained fellow graduate students to develop their science communication skills.[213]

During her STEMprov workshops, Bennett maintains a scientific mindset of curiosity and information gathering. Ever the researcher, she observes her participants and then asks, "Is this helping you?" and "What's working?" "It's like my mad scientist laboratory," Bennett joked.[214] As for her hypothesis that improv provides an adaptable framework for science communication, Bennett thinks it holds true.

"Improv requires you to understand group dynamics, tell stories, and say yes in the face of the unknown. In many

211 Ibid.
212 Ibid.
213 "Nichole Bennett," LinkedIn, accessed November 21, 2020.
214 Nichole Bennett, "STEMprov on Austin Public."

ways, improv draws upon the very same skills we cultivate as science and tech professionals," her STEMprov website declares.[215]

In April 2020, I decided to try out one of Bennett's workshops myself. A dozen or so scientists met virtually, and Bennett had us start out with a simple warm-up that doubled as an icebreaker: pick up an object in the room that was meaningful to us at present and explain its significance. I held up a handcrafted Bolesławiec teacup a colleague had brought me from Poland, while others held up pets and plants, books and instruments, tools and trinkets, and more.

Ultimately, we split into smaller breakout groups to provide elevator pitch–length overviews of our research. In a virtual format, we were not able to move about in space the way I was accustomed to in a typical improv class, but the workshop got at the heart of what is needed for good communication. It reminded me to view the other participants not only as scientists but also as humans with emotions, imaginations, and quirks. Keeping in mind the duality of commonality and divergence made it easier, in turn, to remind myself to speak in a way that would make sense to the humans behind those screens.

As I was speaking about what kind of research I have specialized in, I kept that teacup in mind. With the teacup, certain parts of my story had been self-evident (I used the teacup to drink tea) and some had required additional explanation (for me, teatime signified routine, tradition, and connection amid

---

215 "STEMprov on Austin Public."

the unpredictability, upheaval, and isolation of the COVID-19 pandemic). While talking about my research, I thought about which of my statements needed no elaboration—which of them could stand on their own, like a teacup simply being held up to the screen—and which needed additional details or a backstory.

***

By rendering complex and dynamic scientific processes and abstract mathematical concepts more tangible, and rooting science communication in storytelling skills, the arts help bridge gaps between scientists in different disciplines and make the sciences more approachable and absorbable for non-scientists.

CHAPTER 7:

ART FOR ENHANCED HEALTHCARE

___

The poets did well to conjoin music and medicine, in Apollo, because the office of medicine is but to tune the curious harp of man's body and reduce it to harmony.

-FRANCIS BACON, PHILOSOPHER, SCIENTIST,

AND AUTHOR (1561–1626)

In Greek and Roman antiquity, Apollo—one of twelve mythical figures inhabiting Mount Olympus—was represented as the deity of music, dance, poetry, and healing.[216]

In the classical version of the Hippocratic Oath, which began in the name of "Apollo Physician," the healing profession was referred to as an "art," never a "science." By 1964, Dr. Louis Lasagna, the dean of the School of Medicine at Tufts

---

216 *Encyclopaedia Britannica Online*, Academic ed., s.v. "Apollo," accessed October 3, 2020.

University, had composed a new Hippocratic Oath adapted for the modern practice of medicine. The modern version of the Hippocratic Oath, which is used in many medical schools today, has new doctors pronounce, "I will remember that there is art to medicine as well as science, and that warmth, sympathy, and understanding may outweigh the surgeon's knife or the chemist's drug."[217]

***

To understand more about the scientific and artistic aspects of medicine, I called up my longtime friend and fellow Georgetown University graduate Hemal Sampat, MD, who is an internist and pediatrician at Massachusetts General Hospital and an instructor at Harvard Medical School.

"Medicine is based in science, but it's far more than just science," he told me.

Dr. Sampat explained that medicine has become an increasingly scientific practice over time:

"Especially in the last one hundred years or so, and really in the post–World War II era—ever since we developed penicillin and antibiotics—medicine has become really scientific. In the last one hundred years, we have had some really big breakthroughs in both surgery and medicine that have transformed medicine altogether—especially vaccines, antibiotics, and clean water."

---

217 William C. Shiel, Jr., "Medical Definition of Hippocratic Oath," MedicineNet, accessed November 14, 2020.

As a result, medical admissions and medical training place a premium on scientific aptitude. Sampat noted a contradiction: while in theory, medical schools profess to seek "well-rounded" applicants, in practice, admissions factors are weighted in favor of more lopsided candidates.

"Medical school admissions tests favor those who are very good at processing information the way a computer is—but if you really want to be good at working with patients, you can't be a computer. You have to be able to appreciate psychology, the cultural context a patient comes from, international and local history, and the impact that they have on health and the social determinants of health," Sampat argued.

"You have to be able to—frankly—shoot the [breeze] with patients and hold a conversation with them. You have to be very perceptive and understand when patients have something they are not telling you, when they are telling you one thing but they mean something else, or when their tone of voice suggests that they are telling you what they think you want to hear versus the truth," he continued.

According to Sampat, "You can't just show compassion; you have to feel it. One of the only ways to appreciate their experiences is if you have other [non-medical] experiences. In the scientific way of thinking, you process information by intellectualizing and weighing options by looking at pros and cons. Yet for most people, [medical decision-making has] a much more emotional component to it, and they do not follow this approach of strict intellectualization. Doctors need to appreciate those differences."

The solution, according to Dr. Sampat, is to embrace interdisciplinarity: "Creativity in how you treat someone, diagnose someone, or convey information comes from wide exposure to different disciplines. The most successful doctor is someone who is something of a Renaissance [person]."

***

Pairing a robust scientific approach with knowledge and skills from other disciplines has great potential to increase creativity, communication, and compassion in the context of healthcare. Beyond having well-rounded medical professionals in the healthcare system, the direct integration of literary, visual, and musical arts into medicine can also improve medical training and healthcare delivery.

THE OPERATING THEATER

In the medical field, the operating room is sometimes referred to as the operating theater—in other words, the facility in a hospital where surgeries are performed. On a typical day at the Georgetown University Medical Center, the W. Proctor Harvey Clinical Training Amphitheater is an operating theater in the traditional medical sense. Yet once a year, it is transformed into theater in the artistic sense and becomes a stage for an evening of multiple medicine-themed skits.

This annual "Heart of the Harvey" event is the brainchild of a pair of Georgetown faculty members from two very different corners of campus: neuroscience professor Dr. Bill Rebeck and performing arts professor Susan Lynskey. While few people would bat an eyelid upon learning Professor Lynskey holds a master of fine arts (MFA) degree, it might come as quite a surprise that Professor Rebeck does too.

In the midst of the demands of teaching and researching in his primary professional field at Georgetown, Rebeck earned an MFA from Lesley University in 2015, and when he is not publishing research papers on the molecular mechanisms of Alzheimer's disease, he is writing plays. Rebeck is confident he is not alone in that respect and has affirmed that "a lot of scientists have artistic bents." In his opinion, "Art and medicine draw on similar skills, like using your imagination. But they also draw on different parts of the brain, which can be satisfying."[218]

Indeed, medicine is both a science and an art, yet medical training focuses intensely on the human body while often neglecting the human spirit. The grueling and intensely competitive preparation for a limited number of post-graduation residency positions puts pressure on medical students across the United States to stay hyper-focused on their medical training at the expense of their other interests. The result is competition, isolation, and burnout during what one Georgetown student has called the "wonderful yet harrowing experience" of medical school.[219] Medical students and faculty also tend to have limited outlets to decompress from the stressors they internalize on a daily basis while working closely with injured and ill patients in a clinical setting.

218 Leigh Ann Renzulli, "'Heart of the Harvey' Explores the Intersection of Art and Medicine," Georgetown University, April 3, 2016, accessed October 3, 2020.
219 Kate Zambon, "Putting the Heart in 'The Heart of the Harvey,'" Georgetown University, April 9, 2017, accessed August 31, 2020.

Thus, while Rebeck and Lynskey conceived of the "Heart of the Harvey" as an educational endeavor to "bring scientific principles to the larger public in enjoyable ways," their initiative was also inspired in large part "by the simple existential question of why we are all here."[220]

The "Heart of the Harvey" proved to be a balm for medical students who were eager to tap into their artistic and creative sides. It also served as a bridge between the medical center and other parts of the university campus.

"Our university has had an interest for some time in bringing the main campus and the medical school together more closely," Lynskey revealed. "This seemed to me an extraordinary way to do it."[221]

Members of all parts of the university community were invited to send in short plays examining medically pertinent issues ranging from digital automation to healthcare affordability. Lynskey, for example, performed in *Placebo Control*, a play Rebeck wrote about a pair of laboratory mice contemplating their role in research.[222]

"We asked students, faculty, and staff across campuses to write and submit ten-minute plays," Rebeck explained. "We really wanted a good cross-section of people involved. We

220 Kate Zambon, "Making Space for the Soul at the Heart of the Harvey," Georgetown University, April 16, 2018, accessed August 31, 2020.

221 Renzulli, "'Heart of the Harvey' Explores the Intersection of Art and Medicine."

222 Zambon, "Making Space for the Soul at the Heart of the Harvey."

chose plays from the medical center, main campus, and the School of Continuing Studies."[223]

The success of the initial evening of medical theater was so great the co-founders decided to make it an annual event. Interest in the "Heart of the Harvey" grew across multiple sectors of campus, and the organizers received so many compelling submissions for the second year of the event that they were forced to turn many of them down.[224]

Thanks to Rebeck and Lynskey's creative vision and the enthusiastic response from the medical school and greater university community, medical students have the chance each year to examine healthcare issues through the lens of theater while delivering both entertainment and education to the general public.

"The students, faculty, and staff who participate each year have such inquiry and dedication, and in doing this work, we always learn something new about art, about medicine, [about] self, and about others," Lynskey affirmed.[225]

Perhaps the greatest transformation the "Heart of the Harvey" enables is alluded to in its very name. In Lynskey's words, the core of the initiative is "examining the human condition, the human heart, by teaching and learning empathy and fostering an appreciation for difference—one play at a time."[226]

223 Renzulli, "'Heart of the Harvey' Explores the Intersection of Art and Medicine."
224 Zambon, "Putting the Heart in 'The Heart of the Harvey.'"
225 Ibid.
226 Ibid.

NARRATIVE MEDICINE

Dr. Rita Charon has also placed an understanding of the human condition at the center of her medical practice, and in doing so, has created a new subfield of medicine.

Charon, who said she "got into medicine through the door of activism," spent her college years and mid-twenties questioning and reforming the status quo through the civil rights movement, the anti-war movement, and the feminist movement in the late 1960s and early 1970s. Perhaps it should not be surprising then that, after graduating from Harvard Medical School in 1974, she began to question and reform the existing model of practicing medicine.[227]

After completing her residency, Charon became a primary care physician with Columbia University, practicing in the multiethnic neighborhood of Washington Heights in the New York City borough of Manhattan. As a medical provider, she believed her primary responsibility to her patients was "to listen to what they said and to take in whatever account they came to the doctor's office to give."[228]

"I came to medicine because I was a lifelong reader ... and as a reader, I understood that once I opened my practice, ... what patients paid me to do was to pay exquisite attention to the narratives that they gave me ... and that it was my task to cohere these stories so that they, at least provisionally, made some sense, to take these multiple contradictory narratives

---

227 Lance Weiler, "'Creating a Clearing'—Dr. Rita Charon on the Power of Narrative Medicine," Medium, September 20, 2017, accessed November 14, 2020.
228 Ibid.

and let them build something that we could act on," Charon elaborated.[229]

Her assumptions stood in stark contrast to what she had learned in medical school, which she described as "a reductionist, positivist, disease-centered model" of obtaining a patient's history. Charon's desire to try a "whole other way of using [herself] as a personal instrument" led her to reach out to the faculty of Columbia University's English department, since she "figured they were the ones on campus who knew something about listening to stories."[230]

"I went to the English department and I said, 'Could you teach a doctor something about stories and how they work?' and God bless them, the English department was very happy to take me in," Charon recounted.[231]

Although her original intent had been to take just one English course, her involvement with the English department turned into much more.

"They said, 'Don't take a course. Take a master's,' which I did. And then they said, 'Don't just take a master's. Take a PhD,' which I did," Charon recalled.[232]

---

229 Rita Charon, "Honoring the Stories of Illness | Dr. Rita Charon | TEDx-Atlanta," TEDx Talks, November 4, 2011, YouTube video, 18:16.

230 Weiler, "'Creating a Clearing'—Dr. Rita Charon on the Power of Narrative Medicine."

231 Charon, "Honoring the Stories of Illness | Dr. Rita Charon | TEDxAtlanta."

232 Weiler, "'Creating a Clearing'—Dr. Rita Charon on the Power of Narrative Medicine."

As Charon awakened and nourished her own sense of story, her medical practice was deeply transformed.

"As I learned to read closely, where every word counts, I was able to learn to listen closely, where every word counts. So, in the office, when I saw a new patient, I wouldn't ask millions of questions anymore," said Charon. "I learned not to do that and instead to say, 'I will be your doctor, and so I need to know a great deal about your body and your health and your life. Please tell me what you think I should know about your situation.'" Then she would let her patients simply answer and, without writing down or typing up anything, she would absorb the stories they told her.[233]

As Charon herself acknowledged, her integration of narratology into clinical practice was not the first instance of medicine being brought into conversation with literary studies. Dr. Robert Coles, who began his career as a child psychiatrist, found his life's work as a "cross between doctor, poet, and documentarian," creating "a version of documentary child psychiatry" by recording how social and economic forces affected the mental lives of individuals.[234] Yet Charon's approach is perhaps unique in terms of its practical applications within a traditional clinical context.

"I was by no means the first person to bring literary studies into the practice of medicine," Charon acknowledged, "but somehow, by starting as a doctor first and then getting all

233 Charon, "Honoring the Stories of Illness | Dr. Rita Charon | TEDxAtlanta."
234 Shekerjian, *Uncommon Genius: How Great Ideas Are Born*, 169.

this training in stories and how to understand them, ... my sleeves were more rolled up in using this knowledge."[235]

Charon found her colleagues in the English department to be valuable supporters of her patient-centered approach to medicine, saying, "I think they really joined me in the idea that the knowledge they had—very specialized narratological knowledge—could do something good in the world."[236]

Immediately after earning her PhD in English in 1999, Charon began drawing together experts and artists from many disciplines—"literary scholars, philosophers, oral historians, psychiatrists, psychoanalysts, pediatricians, novelists"—to develop "a rigorous model of theory and practice for how a clinician can hear what a patient tells him or her." In 2000, she coined the term "narrative medicine" to describe the new field they were pioneering.[237]

Charon has defined narrative medicine as "clinical practice fortified by the knowledge of what to do with stories."[238] She equates that knowledge with the ability to "recognize when someone is telling you a story" and to "absorb the story" as a "whole," not only through words but also through unsaid hints such as silences and facial expressions. The physician's role, according to Charon, is to "absorb" those hints,

235 Charon, "Honoring the Stories of Illness | Dr. Rita Charon | TEDxAtlanta."
236 Ibid.
237 Weiler, "'Creating a Clearing'—Dr. Rita Charon on the Power of Narrative Medicine."
238 Charon, "Honoring the Stories of Illness | Dr. Rita Charon | TEDxAtlanta."

to "interpret them," to "honor them," and "to be moved by them to action."[239]

Charon is now professor of medicine and founder and executive director of the Program in Narrative Medicine at Columbia University, where master of science students follow a pioneering curriculum that combines narrative writing and close reading skills, literary and philosophical analysis, and experiential work in clinical and educational settings. The core curriculum of the program draws together literary, sociological, and psychological theories in courses including Giving and Receiving Accounts of Self; Illness and Disability Narratives: Embodiment, Community, Activism; The Self and Other in the Clinical Encounter; Methods of Narrative Medicine; and Applied Writing in the Narrative Medicine Context and Beyond.[240]

In the two decades since Charon first began navigating and defining the concept, narrative medicine has become a fully developed subfield of medicine. The narrative medicine program at Columbia has trained 150 doctors, nurses, and chaplains to date.[241] Similar programs have also been established at other highly regarded institutions of higher education, including the University of Southern California, the University of Arizona, and Temple University.

Most importantly, narrative medicine has had a real impact on patient care. Several studies have shown that narrative

239 Ibid.
240 "Narrative Medicine," Columbia University, accessed September 24, 2020.
241 Sigal Samuel, "This Doctor Is Taking Aim at Our Broken Medical System, One Story at a Time," Vox, March 5, 2020, accessed September 24, 2020.

training helps doctors better understand, empathize with, and communicate with their patients—in medical specialties ranging from genetics counseling to fetal cardiology to surgical training. [242, 243, 244, 245, 246, 247] In 2016, a systematic review found that narrative medicine has been "a powerful instrument for decreasing pain and increasing well-being related to illness."[248, 249]

VISUAL BODY MAPPING FOR HIV CARE

On the other side of the globe, South African researcher Dr. Annabelle Wienand has drawn upon the visual arts to advance the state of healthcare. As a master's student in the University of Cape Town's AIDS and Society Research Unit (ASRU), Wienand saw a need for increased awareness of

242 David Garrison et al., "Qualitative Analysis of Medical Student Impressions of a Narrative Exercise in the Third-Year Psychiatry Clerkship," *Academic Medicine* 86 no. 1 (January 2011): 85–89.

243 Mordechai Muszkat et al., "Teaching Empathy through Poetry: An Clinically Based Model," *Medical Education* 44 (2010): 489–526.

244 Shannon L. Arntfield et al., "Narrative Medicine as a Means of Training Medical Students toward Residency Competencies," *Patient Education and Counseling* 91 no. 3 (June 2013): 280–286.

245 Małgorzata J. M. Nowaczyk, "Narrative Medicine in Clinical Genetics Practice," *American Journal of Medical Genetics, Part A* 158A no. 8 (August 2012): 1941–1947.

246 Sarah Chambers and Julie Glickstein, "Making a Case for Narrative Competency in the Field of Fetal Cardiology," *Literature and Medicine* 29 no. 2 (Fall 2011): 376–395.

247 A. Scott Pearson et al., "Narrative Medicine in Surgical Education," *Journal of Surgical Education* 65 no. 2 (March–April 2008): 99–100.

248 Chiara Fioretti et al., "Research Studies on Patients' Illness Experience Using the Narrative Medicine Approach: A Systematic Review," *BMJ Open* 6 (2016).

249 Samuel, "This Doctor is Taking Aim at our Broken Medical System, One Story at a Time."

human biology among patients participating in HIV literacy training and their caregivers.

To address this need, she had a tradition of HIV-related arts to draw upon. In the 1990s, a group of HIV-positive mothers in Uganda had started creating memory boxes and memory books for their children. The mothers decorated and filled these boxes and books with important documents, photographs, pictures, and stories of their lives. These artistic creations were a means for the mothers to disclose their HIV-positive status to their children and open a delicate conversation about planning for the future. Wienand took inspiration from the memory boxes and books as a way of encouraging people to "think critically, develop new understanding, and ultimately live informed and positive lives" within an HIV-related health context.[250]

Adopting and refining an HIV-themed visual storytelling approach, Wienand built upon a body mapping activity her colleagues at ASRU had developed for the Life Long Project, an initiative for women living with HIV launched in 2002 by Drs. Jonathan Morgan and Kylie Thomas in association with the international humanitarian medical non-governmental organization Médecins Sans Frontières (Doctors Without Borders). In the Life Long Project body mapping activity, the participating women were invited to incorporate visual representations of their bodies—and the effects of HIV upon their bodies—into personal storytelling; thirteen women from the Bambanani Women's Group met over three

---

250 "Mapping Our Lives: Mapping Workshop Manual," University of Cape Town, April 2007.

months with artist Jane Soloman to create life-size drawings that recorded their journey of living with HIV.[251]

Wienand combined her expertise in the visual arts and her skills in health curriculum development to expand upon this body mapping concept in design workshops, enabling participants to engage in visual storytelling for health literacy training. In her workshops, participants traced outlines of one another's bodies onto giant pieces of paper and then engaged in a series of interactive exercises to create life-size drawings of their bodies while thinking about, discussing, and understanding how their life story and HIV had affected their bodies.[252]

These "body map drawings" helped the participants to expand their knowledge of human biology in relation to HIV prevention, care, and treatment. Just as significantly, the visual medium gave participants a comfortable forum for exchanging their personal stories and experiences with HIV. The life-size drawings created in the visual body mapping workshops thus contributed to improved healthcare delivery by increasing the scientific knowledge of patients, individuals involved in their care, and the community at large.

These visual creations even gained recognition as valuable pieces of artwork. With the permission of the workshop participants who created the body maps, the life-size drawings were exhibited in 2002 at the South African National Gallery in Cape Town, as well as in London and New York. The

---

251 Ibid.
252 Ibid.

original body maps were then auctioned, and limited edition prints of the originals were produced. The proceeds from the sale of the prints, which are now part of collections in museums, art galleries, and private homes, were donated to HIV/AIDS organizations in South Africa.[253]

Since Wienand introduced visual body mapping workshops in South Africa, visual body mapping has been used across the globe for a variety of purposes, including advocacy and therapy in Kenya, women's health activism in Japan, examination of students' rights in Colombia, and nurses' training in Canada.[254]

CUSTOMIZABLE 3D-PRINTED PROSTHETIC DESIGN

Winston Frazer, a creative entrepreneur and graduate of the Maryland Institute College of Art (MICA), also brought his passion for art into the medical sector. He founded Danae Prosthetics, a start-up company based in Baltimore, Maryland, to enable individuals with lower-limb amputations to take part in designing and creating covers for their own prosthetic devices.

"We are the design house for humanity," Frazer said of Danae Prosthetics.[255]

---

253 "Visual Body Maps and 'Mapping Our Lives,'" University of Cape Town, accessed September 24, 2020.

254 Denise Gastaldo et al., "Body-Map Storytelling as a Health Research Methodology: Blurred Lines Creating Clear Pictures," *Forum Qualitative Sozialforschung / Forum: Qualitative Social Research* 19 no. 2, art. 3 (May 2018).

255 "Tech25," *Washington Life*, February 2019, 40.

His business idea arose out of his personal interactions with residents of São Tomé and Príncipe during a trip he took with a MICA professor to the African island nation. While he was there, he noticed a significant portion of the population was impacted by amputation.[256] During a hospital stay, he met several São Toméans with amputated limbs. He was moved by their confessions to him of the self-consciousness and ostracization accompanying their condition.[257] At the same time, they inspired him with their resilience and optimism.

"The Islanders were happy, expressive, and full of life. They embraced their circumstance and focused more on what life had to offer, instead of looking at what they had lost. This dramatically changed my outlook on life and filled me with hope and inspiration," Frazer said in an interview with *SciArt Magazine*.[258]

Inspired by their "unshakeable will," Frazer decided to help patients like them by combining his interests in digital fabrication and the visual arts to create original, customizable, and affordable prosthetic devices.[259] He developed the concept for Danae Prosthetics as part of his undergraduate thesis.

"I was later encouraged to bring this idea to the world because the amputation community needed a fresh perspective in an

---

256 Danielle McCloskey, "An Interview with Danae Prosthetics' CEO Winston Frazer," *SciArt Magazine*, April 2018, accessed October 20, 2020.
257 Jonathan M. Pitts, "Baltimore Startup Blends Art and Technology in Helping Amputees Design Personalized Prosthetic Covers," *The Baltimore Sun,* April 6, 2018, accessed September 24, 2020.
258 McCloskey, "An Interview with Danae Prosthetics' CEO Winston Frazer."
259 "Tech25."

industry that lacked diversity, variety, and flair," Frazer told *SciArt Magazine.*[260]

After graduating with a degree in painting, Frazer participated in MICA's Up/Start Venture Competition and won a twenty-five-thousand-dollar award, which he used to found Danae.

Users can upload the shape and dimension of their prosthetic devices to an app and then provide whatever design they choose to be 3D-printed into customized prosthetic covers. By personalizing the look of their prostheses, said Frazer, Danae's clientele can use their devices as an outlet for aesthetic expression, which in turn helps relieve some social stresses about their physical condition.

"When creative and scientific approaches come together, you're going to do better, more meaningful work," Frazer told *The Baltimore Sun.*[261]

POINT MOTION: A MUSICAL TOOL, FOR QUANTIFIED OUTCOMES

In addition to the visual arts, music is commonly integrated into healthcare. Although music therapy as an allied health profession did not formally emerge until the late eighteenth

260 McCloskey, "An Interview with Danae Prosthetics' CEO Winston Frazer."
261 Pitts, "Baltimore Startup Blends Art and Technology in Helping Amputees Design Personalized Prosthetic Covers."

century, traditional forms of musical healing are thought to have ancient roots.[262]

As medicine and technology advance, the ways in which they can be combined with music are also evolving. A recent example is Point Motion, a musical tool for quantified health outcomes I learned about through my involvement with the Center for Transformative Technology, a Silicon Valley–based non-profit organization that connects, educates, and inspires a worldwide community of innovators creating technological solutions to elevate mental and emotional well-being.

Speaking at a virtual Transformative Technology event, Point Motion's CEO and founder Kevin Clark and chief strategy officer Imen Maaroufi presented a patented motion-control technology that allows users to create music through their own body movements. They demonstrated to attendees an example of a memory test in which a movement is assigned arbitrarily to a specific image, and the user's task is to remember which movement corresponds with which image.[263]

"Arms straight up," announced the supportive narration, accompanied by a demonstration of the movement, as an image of a dog simultaneously appeared. Behind my screen, I lifted my arms while thinking about man's best friend. "Crossing arms," sounded the next verbal cue, as the

262 *Encyclopaedia Britannica Online*, Academic ed., s.v. "Music therapy," accessed October 15, 2020.

263 Kevin Clark and Imen Maaroufi, "Point Motion: A Musical Tool, for Quantified Outcomes," virtual presentation and discussion hosted by the Transformative Technology Community, October 15, 2020.

photograph of the dog was replaced by one of a cat. "Flexing arms," we then heard, as the image of a horse appeared.[264]

Actual users of this program, they explained, would be asked to repeat the movements with the supportive narration and animal images but no movement demonstration. Next, the verbal prompt would be removed. Meanwhile, the program would be measuring their reaction time, using all of this information to quickly generate a report of quantifiable data on physical and cognitive performance.[265]

The data could then be accessed to see how frequently users had been participating in such exercises, how much time they had spent on them, how their reaction times had changed over time, and which cues or movements they were not responding to. In that way, Point Motion is "very supplemental and very enhancing to care programs," Clark explained, because it creates "digital experience workstations that allow pen-and-paper assessments to be transformed into interactive exercises people do at home."[266]

"None of this is to replace the therapist," Maaroufi clarified; rather, its purpose is to "create non-invasive ways of measuring wellness" with quantified outcomes and a focus on early detection. "Humans are living longer, but are they living better?" she asked. By proactively measuring "continuous growth"—in other words, by focusing on what happens

---

264 Ibid.
265 Ibid.
266 Ibid.

between doctors' visits—Point Motion aims to improve the human healthspan.[267]

As questions about the technology itself arose, Clark noted that none of the Point Motion technology is "out-of-the-box" software. Rather, Point Motion allows care providers to create customized curriculum packages in a "very intuitive process," akin to how a musician might use a digital audio workstation to create music.[268]

Clark, a graduate of the Berklee College of Music, personally developed Point Motion's unique technology with the aim of using his music training for good. "I wanted to use music in a way that could make the best impact, and I knew that just writing another song wasn't going to do that," he shared. What was going to make an impact, he believed, would be "using music to produce a better quality of life for people."[269]

Although founding a health and education software company might seem like a daunting endeavor for a musician, Clark had the traits of patience and determination on his side. "I was denied two years in a row from going to Berklee. It took me three years to get there," he stated emphatically. His persistence paid off, and in 2015, he graduated with a double major in jazz composition and film scoring.[270] When it came to his career path, though, he maintained a flexible outlook.[271]

---

267 Ibid.
268 Ibid.
269 Ibid.
270 "The Team," Point Motion, accessed November 14, 2020.
271 Ibid.

Surrounded by incredibly talented musicians, he thought, *I am going to go hungry if I depend on my piano-playing abilities.* He then asked himself, *What am I good at?* Upon reflection, he realized he was excellent at "seeing where people had special talent and writing music that highlighted that talent."[272]

As a technological entrepreneur, Clark ended up relying on that same knack for using his creativity to draw out others' talents. "We want everyone to be an expert at what they do," Clark stated, as he explained the impact Point Motion has had thus far. It has been used to benefit physical therapy and rehabilitation, the treatment of Parkinson's disease, neurodiverse communities such as individuals on the autism spectrum, and early education programs in school districts serving children with special needs. Its geographical reach extends from the United States and Canada to Australia.[273]

***

From narrative medicine to visual body mapping to music-infused healthcare technology, art can increase provider and patient competency and communication, thereby improving healthcare delivery, lengthening life expectancies, and saving lives.

---

272 Ibid.
273 Ibid.

PART III:

SCIENCES AND ARTS
ADVANCE HUMANITY

CHAPTER 8:

ART AS SCIENCE AND TECHNOLOGY ACTIVISM

———

Art is activism.

-ANGIE THOMAS, NOVELIST (1988–PRESENT)

Art has long been known to have many of the elements essential to inspiring social change. It has the power to move people emotionally.[274] It grabs our attention and sinks into our memory. It invites us to look at the world in ways we have never seen it—or to take a longer look in ways we once glimpsed but then brushed away and quickly forgot.

According to art education professor Dr. Melody Milbrandt, "the arts give voice and form to individual and collective needs that motivate and sustain social movements." They can "reinforce values of the group, raise questions about current

---

274 Alex Neill, "Art and Emotion," in *The Oxford Handbook of Aesthetics*, ed. Jerrold Levinson (Oxford: Oxford University Press, 2003), 421–435.

social conditions, and construct an image of social change," and they "often challenge dominant ideas, values, and tactics" by "evoking emotions and meanings not easily reduced to narrow ideological terms."[275]

Art combined with technology and science can be an especially powerful vehicle for activism. Art can speak directly to societal concerns related to science and technology. Technology can also be infused into art to make that message more compelling.

DIGITAL ARTS RECONSTRUCTION AND DECOLONIZATION

Thousands of years before the modern boundaries of Iraq were drawn, Mesopotamia—the lands between the Tigris and Euphrates Rivers—was the cradle of some of the world's earliest civilizations, including the Assyrian Empire. In what is now Iraq's Nineveh Governorate once lay Hatra, a fortified caravan city that flourished in the second century CE.

It was not until the mid-twentieth century that systematic excavation of the impressive ruins of Hatra took place. In 1951, Iraqi archaeologists began the delicate process of uncovering Hatrene artifacts, including a dozen ancient Mesopotamian shrines and hundreds of stone statues and statuettes.[276]

---

275 Melody K. Milbrandt, "Understanding the Role of Art in Social Movements and Transformation," *Journal of Art for Life* 1 no. 1 (2010): 8–9, 13.
276 *Encyclopaedia Iranica Online*, Academic ed., s.v. "Hatra," accessed March 9, 2021.

In 2015, in stark contrast, ISIS militants entered the Mosul Museum in northern Iraq and began the indelicate process of hammering into pieces Assyrian and Hatrene artifacts, on the premise that they were symbols of idolatry. These antiquities, after surviving centuries under various powers that had ruled or sought to conquer the land on which they stood, were lost to the world in a matter of minutes.[277]

As videos of the destruction in the Mosul Museum emerged and circulated, many observers across the globe watched in outrage. Activist and media artist Morehshin Allahyari resolved to take action, determined to prevent these cultural artifacts from being forgotten. She began researching the sculptures with the intention of recreating each of them digitally. Her digital reconstruction of the artifacts was, on one hand, an act of defiance against ISIS, said Allahyari, but it was also "a gesture for these things to be remembered."[278]

For Allahyari, who was born and raised in Iran, the work was also a way of honoring the historical connections between parts of the modern-day Middle East, such as Iran and Iraq, that are divided by conflict. The artifacts, which date back 2,500 or 3,000 years, harken to a time "when history was shared between all these countries," Allahyari said.[279]

277 Christopher Jones, "Assessment of the ISIS Destruction at the Mosul Museum," Ancient History Et Cetera, March 9, 2015, accessed August 24, 2020.

278 Oliver Franklin-Wallis, "Defying Daesh—with a 3D Printer," Wired, March 19, 2017, accessed August 24, 2020.

279 Adizah Eghan, "Artist Uses 3D Tech to Recreate Past Destroyed by ISIS," KQED, January 14, 2016, accessed August 29, 2020.

As a resident artist at the software company Autodesk in San Francisco, Allahyari had ready access to 3D-modeling and -printing technologies. Yet the process of digitally reconstructing the artifacts was far from easy. While gathering information online, she found that information in Farsi-language websites differed from that in Arabic websites, which in turn conflicted with the information available in English. Because of these discrepancies, it took her a year to finish the data-collection portion of the research process.[280]

Furthermore, the lack of available images of the artifacts complicated the 3D modeling process. Allahyari had access to seven to ten high-quality images per artifact on average, whereas twenty-five to thirty photographs taken from different angles are generally needed as input for the software to create a reliable 3D model. Faced with a dearth of visual data, Allahyari ended up creating 3D models from scratch.[281]

Meanwhile, organizations such as US-based digital archiver Cyark were also working to digitally recreate the destroyed artifacts and make them available digitally—but only by purchase. The foreign commercialization of digitally recreated artifacts irked Allahyari, who saw the destruction of cultural heritage and the appropriation of cultural heritage as two sides of the same coin.

"If ISIS takes over this ownership of cultural heritage by destruction," she said, "the other side of it is this simplistic,

280 Morehshin Allahyari, "Morehshin Allahyari: On Digital Colonialism, Re-figuring, and Monstrosity," UM Stamps, November 7, 2017, YouTube video, 59:12.
281 Ibid.

utopian Silicon Valley [approach]. Their claim is, 'We are saving the cultural heritage of the world'—actually, you are selling a product."[282]

Allahyari resolved she, in contrast, would make her own digital recreations freely accessible.

"It's about ownership," she explained. "It's about taking the ownership of digital data as seriously as the physical." She worked with the New Museum of Contemporary Art in Manhattan and Rhizome, its affiliated digital art organization, to release a folder containing all the research she had gathered on the artifacts.[283]

In March 2017, the FACT gallery in Liverpool, England, featured an exhibit of Allahyari's work called *Material Speculation: ISIS* that included 3D-printed replicas of twelve destroyed artifacts. The sculptures included human figures, such as King Uthal of Hatra, as well as representations of ancient Mesopotamian deities, such as the human-headed winged bull Lamassu.[284]

In each of the sculptures, Allahyari had embedded a USB key containing the digital files for the artifact. She explained in a public talk that inside each object, "I have embedded a memory card or flash drive that contains all the information that I have gathered around the artifacts: images, PDF files, my email correspondence, the process of making the work,

---

282 Franklin-Wallis, "Defying Daesh—with a 3D Printer."
283 Ibid.
284 Ibid.

and also STL or OBJ files, which are standard 3D-print files, of all the models."[285]

To access the files from the works of art, Allahyari stressed, "You don't have to destroy them." The digital files are tucked away in the back of each sculpture and sealed off with resin, and thus accessible at any time deemed appropriate to break the seal.[286]

"The idea was really to think about these sculptures as time capsules. Time capsules should be kept for the future civilizations," as a way to "resist that forgetting of memory," she explained.[287]

CLIMATE-AWARENESS AUGMENTED REALITY MURAL

Social entrepreneur Linda Cheung has also used art as a call to draw attention to a matter of pressing concern: the global climate change crisis. Cheung is the founder and creative director of Before It's Too Late (BITL), a Miami-based non-profit organization that uses arts and technology to "awaken and inspire people to take action on climate change."[288]

Cheung creates technology-infused art as a call to action, in a significant shift from her initial approach to addressing the environmental crisis. Cheung confessed to PBS special correspondent Alicia Menendez that, before becoming an artist

285 Allahyari, "Morehshin Allahyari: On Digital Colonialism, Re-figuring, and Monstrosity."
286 Ibid.
287 Ibid.
288 Before It's Too Late, accessed August 29, 2020.

in Miami, she "used to scoff at art." Working in finance on Wall Street after earning her master of business administration (MBA) from the Massachusetts Institute of Technology (MIT), she did not picture herself painting in Miami's famed mural district.[289]

"For me, everything was about numbers," recounted Cheung, who initially saw the environmental crisis as a "systems problem." She believed the solution was "policy change" and "investment dollars," until she was struck by a new realization: "The problem is cultural."[290]

Cheung decided to increase climate literacy by creating public murals infused with augmented reality technology—but she knew she could not do it alone.

"I had to meet and find out who the best muralists were in Wynwood and find a wall. How do you do augmented reality? I needed to find someone who did augmented reality programming," Cheung recounted.[291] Enter programmer and digital designer Juan Carlos Gallo, with whom Cheung collaborated to create a pilot augmented reality mural entitled *What Future Do You Choose for Miami?*

The pilot mural, unveiled in February 2018, showed "Miami's vibrant colors, materialism, and party culture as a façade balanced over a looming sea level line," with "warning signs,"

---

289 Alicia Menendez and Lorna Baldwin, "In Miami, How Art Intersects with Technology and Climate Change," *PBS NewsHour*, May 29, 2019, accessed August 24, 2020.

290 Ibid.

291 Ibid.

exemplified by a bright yellow canary, illustrating "ignorance [of] the impending threat." The accompanying augmented reality experience allowed participants to "travel into two alternate futures for Miami," where they were "confronted with the direct question of how they will shape the city's future."[292]

In one future—a grim projection of the scenario in which Miamians have ignored environmental considerations—Miami's skyscrapers tumble into the ocean as the rising sea line creeps above the caged canary and a child's voice asks on behalf of the extinguished lifeforms, "Why couldn't you stop to take care of us? Were your profits so important that you sacrificed what we had?"[293]

The bright scenario, in contrast, presents a thriving city bearing evidence of the behavioral and infrastructural changes Miami's human population has made, such as relying on carbon-free forms of transportation and renewable energy sources, which allow them to live comfortably in their city in harmony with the natural environment.[294]

For the next mural, *Anthropocene Extinction*, artist Reiner Gamboa and musician Dane Myers rounded out the team. *Anthropocene Extinction*, which took over a month and a half to paint and debuted in December 2018, was designed to allow viewers to interact digitally with any of the illustrated

292 "What Future Do You Choose for Miami?" Before It's Too Late, accessed November 14, 2020.

293 Ibid.

294 Ibid.

animals: a black panther, a sea turtle, and a coyote, among others.[295, 296]

In a *PBS NewsHour* feature, Gallo demonstrated the augmented reality experience he had designed. He pointed a Samsung tablet toward a manatee and sea turtle, and a video of a real sea turtle swimming in the ocean popped up on his screen.

"In this case, for example, it recognized the sea turtle's leg, so in this case now, it's playing the sea turtle video," said Gallo. The video cut to footage of bottles, six-pack rings, and other plastic waste littering the sea turtles' marine habitat. "This story is basically telling you how plastic is affecting the ecosystem and how turtles and all kinds of animals are consuming this plastic," he explained.[297]

The mural was painted in bright colors and the intricately depicted animals were beautiful to behold, but the message it sought to convey was stark and somber. Its title, *Anthropocene Extinction*, left no doubt as to the devastating outcome its creators were urging the public to prevent by changing course—before it is too late.

In September 2019, the mural was vandalized with graffiti, which marred the beautiful illustrations and rendered the

295 Before It's Too Late (@bitl.earth), "Yesterday our mural 'Anthropocene Extinction' was severely vandalized [...]," Instagram photo, September 19, 2019.

296 "Anthropocene Extinction," Before It's Too Late, accessed October 18, 2020.

297 Ibid.

augmented reality experience defunct. Before It's Too Late shared the disheartening news of the "heartless destruction of art" on social media, noting that "the beloved mural," which in its "short life" had drawn "thousands of visitors," had been expected to remain on display for another year. The Before It's Too Late team decided not to restore the mural, deciding the mural had, from its start to its end, "served its purpose."[298]

Thanking the public for the "compassion and empathy" they had expressed in condolence messages to Cheung and Gamboa, Before It's Too Late shared the following reflection in an Instagram post:

"While the vandalization of street murals is always a risk, especially in Wynwood, the story we are interested in telling is how the way this mural ended is very much a reflection of its message. Our actions are causing the Sixth Mass Extinction of Biodiversity, without our awareness, love, care, or respect. The true art that is being destroyed is a million times worse than our loss—that of nature, the over two hundred species that took millennia to create that are going extinct every single day. In a way, our mural ended in the most poetic way possible—ahead of its time and sharing the message it intended to share."[299]

Before It's Too Late went on to produce more augmented reality murals, including *Liberty Gardens Park*, which features the interconnectivity of Florida's native trees, plants, and

---

298 Before It's Too Late (@bitl.earth), "Yesterday our mural 'Anthropocene Extinction' was severely vandalized [...]."
299 Ibid.

pollinators, and *Bronzeville Renaissance*, which highlights "African-American life and culture in Chicago" while envisioning rising above the threat of climate change by using "innovation and renewable technologies to build a 'Community of the Future.'"

What drives Cheung in her work is a firm belief that, contrary to public opinion, "care about the environment" and "care about people's economic welfare" go hand in hand.[300] Human-driven environmental degradation and associated crises carry crushing economic and societal costs, and time is of the essence in correcting course. The challenge is getting that message out in an engaging and compelling way.

"I really want to reach more people from the general public, but the bridge to the public is missing," said Cheung, voicing a concern that is common to many changemakers.[301]

She sees art as a key part of the solution: "I think that art can be that bridge."[302]

STUDIOTOPIA'S SCIENTIST IN RESIDENCE

The belief that the arts paired with the sciences can communicate the urgency of sustainable thinking to the public is also what led mechanical and structural engineer DM Hoyt into collaboration with Christiaan Zwanikken, a renowned

300 Ibid.
301 Ibid.
302 Ibid.

artist who divides his time between Amsterdam and a four-hundred-year-old Franciscan monastery in Portugal.

Hoyt is an Amsterdam-based mechanical and structural engineer who describes himself as "a creative pragmatist with a methodical mind and a love for brainstorming." He also happens to be related to me, and in August 2020, he shared with our family the exciting news that he had been selected from over 160 applicants to embark on a two-year "creative journey addressing sustainable development across Europe through the converging views of art and science" as a scientist in residence with STUDIOTOPIA, a European Union–funded, multi-institutional, interdisciplinary initiative to address the United Nations Sustainable Development Goals (SDGs).

For Hoyt, as for many other scientists, art and science have much in common. In his winning application portfolio, he wrote the following:

"Art and science exist at two ends of the same spectrum. I see the creative process and the scientific method inquiry as parallel approaches with not-so-different goals. Art and science both aim to describe, represent, explain, and reflect on various aspects of our reality."

The distinct advantage of the arts, in his opinion, is their ability to inspire the kind of "radical change" needed to attain the SDGs. Whereas "changing people's perception is not the specialty of scientists," artists "have the capacity to distill science down to powerful concepts that touch us in ways that data alone never will," he argued.

He elaborated on this point in a letter to the selection committee:

"I believe that art-science collaboration is needed to magnify messages that can lead to powerful changes in human perception. Engineers can benefit from artistic approaches such as 'reduce, simplify, and abstract' just as artists can benefit from the methods of scientific inquiry to challenge assumptions, validate hypotheses, and distill complex questions down to the solutions we seek. Speculation also has a role in both art and science since expanding our understanding of reality requires contemplation of the unproven. By working together, they have the potential to bring the principles and urgency of sustainable thinking to everyone on the art-science spectrum."

For over twenty years, Hoyt has applied "scientific research to real-world problems with the goal of improving our quality of life and reducing our carbon footprint." As the founder and director of the structural engineering company NSE Composites, he "collaborated with a small team of engineers to solve novel, open-ended design problems focused on optimizing the performance of wind turbines and increasing the fuel-efficiency of airplanes." Previously, he had spent several years participating in a "major evolutionary step forward toward more fuel-efficient aircraft" as a structural engineer at the Boeing Company.

However, Hoyt believed he could do more to help the global community in facing our "unsustainable trajectory."

"While this work helps move us in the right direction, it brings incremental change at best. The reality is, incremental change to the status quo won't get us to our sustainability goals fast enough," he explained.

Thus, he sought to become involved in "creative, cross-disciplinary, and speculative projects that have the potential to move us toward a more sustainable future." He believed his "engineering mindset" would be "useful in transforming scientific research and complex concepts into practical understanding," while art is what would effectively "communicate important messages that bring meaningful change to society."

Hoyt was no stranger to the art world. He had "collaborated with artists, architects, dancers, sculptors, and other creatives on a range of products including large-scale light and sound installations," including *Swing Time*, an immersive video installation simulating the physiological effects of five hundred years of human life on the Moon, which was experienced by tens of thousands of visitors at the *Giant Steps* exhibition in Seattle and won second place in the People's Choice Awards.

"To achieve the radical shifts in behaviors and priorities required to sustain life on Earth, we need powerful, mind-bending experiences that bring our collective desire for survival into focus," Hoyt opined.

Christiaan Zwanikken's work is, in his view, just the type of art to do so:

"It is powerful and surreal enough to shake our perception of reality, while bringing a sense of familiarity to our subconscious. To me, his work evokes a disorienting sense of wonder that promises to transcend the artificial divide between humans and all of the other living beings on the planet with whom we share our evolutionary existence."

***

Whether by using technology to bring the social message of art to life or by using art to shift perceptions and behavior when scientific data alone fails to move people to action, art in combination with science and technology has the potential to move the needle on societal challenges of our time.

CHAPTER 9:

ART AND SCIENCE CULTIVATE AWE

———

*The most beautiful thing we can experience is the mysterious.
It is the source of all true art and science.*

-ALBERT EINSTEIN, PHYSICIST AND NOBEL
PRIZE LAUREATE (1879–1955)

If there is one theme that repeatedly resurfaces in conversations about human contemplation of the sciences and the arts, it is that of awe.

Definitions of awe vary, and the experience of awe is culturally embedded.[303] The Greater Good Science Center at the University of California, Berkeley defines awe as "the feeling we get in the presence of something vast that challenges our understanding of the world." It notes that "when people feel

———

303 Jennifer Stellar, "How Culture Shapes the Experience of Awe," *Greater Good Magazine*, accessed March 6, 2021.

awe, they may use other words to describe the experience, such as wonder, amazement, surprise, or transcendence."[304] What psychologists call "awe" corresponds very closely to what philosophers refer to as "the sublime."[305]

Awe is understood to be central to the human experience and a uniquely human attribute—perhaps *the most* human attribute. As Dr. Dacher Keltner has pointed out, Greek philosopher Protagoras, who lived in the fifth century BCE, argued that the signature strength of humans as a species is our capacity for awe.[306]

Furthermore, the experience of awe holds tremendous benefits for us. Cutting-edge research conducted at the University of California, Berkeley suggests that awe has "profound psychological, social, and physical health benefits—perhaps even stronger, in some cases, than those of other positive emotions."[307] Those benefits include increased prosocial behavior.[308] As Keltner has explained, awe shifts people from focusing on their "self-interest to being really interested in other people" and "more curious about the world."[309] Awe is also the only positive emotion that regulates the human cytokine response, keeping bodily inflammation at healthy

---

304 "What Is Awe?" *Greater Good Magazine*, accessed March 6, 2021.

305 Margherita Arcangeli et al., "Awe and the Experience of the Sublime: A Complex Relationship," *Frontiers in Psychology* 11 (2020): 1340.

306 Ibid.

307 "The Art & Science of Awe," Greater Good Science Center, accessed March 6, 2021.

308 Joshua D. Perlin and Leon Li, "Why Does Awe Have Prosocial Effects? New Perspectives on Awe and the Small Self," *Perspectives on Psychological Science* 15 no. 2 (2020).

309 Ibid.

levels.[310] Keltner has noted that awe is, in many ways, the salve to prevailing cultural malaise, countering self-focus, greed, anomie, stress, and subpar health with an expanded sense of self, generosity, purpose, creativity, and robust health.[311]

Traditionally conceived of solely as a religious or spiritual emotion, awe has also been considered an aesthetic emotion since eighteenth-century philosopher Edmund Burke wrote his treatise *Philosophical Enquiry into the Origin of Our Ideas of the Sublime and Beautiful*, in which he argued that architecture, poetry, and artwork, if they are of sufficient magnitude, magnificence, or grandeur, can evoke the sublime.[312]

Modern-day researchers have also set forth arguments that awe is a scientific emotion. A group of psychology researchers at the University of California, Berkeley noted that "scientists often report that awe motivates them to answer questions about the natural world, and to do so in naturalistic terms"; their study of awe as a scientific emotion found that awe is the only positive emotion associated with scientific thinking.[313]

There appears to be very sparse current research literature about how science and art, specifically in combination with

---

310 Jennifer E. Stellar et al., "Positive Affect and Markers of Inflammation: Discrete Positive Emotions Predict Lower Levels of Inflammatory Cytokines," *Emotion* 15 no. 2 (2015): 129–133.

311 Perlin and Li, "Why Does Awe Have Prosocial Effects? New Perspectives on Awe and the Small Self."

312 Jeff McLaughlin, *The Originals: Classic Readings in Western Philosophy* (Victoria, BC: BCcampus/TRU, 2017).

313 Sara Gottlieb et al., "Awe as a Scientific Emotion," *Cognitive Science* 42 no. 6 (2018).

one another, elicit awe. Nevertheless, multiple individuals at the vanguard of their fields, including both artists and scientists, have identified awe as being at the heart of both art and science.

Nobel laureate poet Derek Walcott said, in a conversation with Denise Shekerjian, the author of *Uncommon Ideas: How Great Ideas Are Born*, "Good science and good art are always about a condition of awe. This may seem to you like a large theme, but the best science and poetry at [their] greatest are not smaller than that. I don't think there is any other function for the poet or the scientist in the human tribe but the astonishment of the soul."[314]

Physicist Dr. Richard Feynman, also a Nobel Prize winner, wrote to artist Jirayr ("Jerry") Zorthian of a "scientific awe" at the scientific laws of nature he longed to be able to communicate through art: "I wanted very much to learn to draw, for a reason that I kept to myself: I wanted to convey an emotion I have about the beauty of the world." Feynman likened this emotion to a religious sentiment, pointing to the feeling that arises "when you think about how things that appear so different and behave so differently are all run 'behind the scenes' by the same organization, the same physical laws." He believed this feeling of "scientific awe" could "be communicated through a drawing to someone who also had that emotion," as a momentary reminder of "this feeling about the glories of the universe."[315]

---

314 Shekerjian, *Uncommon Genius: How Great Ideas Are Born*, 176.
315 Richard P. Feynman, *"Surely You're Joking, Mr. Feynman!" Adventures of a Curious Character* (New York: W. W. Norton & Company, 1997), 237–238.

Dr. Luis Álvarez-Gaumé, a theoretical physicist at the cutting-edge European Organization for Nuclear Research (CERN), has also spoken of "a sense of awe" in science that "art helps bring … to the surface."[316]

Psychologist Dr. Mihaly Csikszentmihalyi has identified some of the fundamental commonalities of the arts and the sciences, which hint at where that awe arises from:

"Nuclear physics, biology, poetry, and musical composition share few symbols and rules, yet the calling for these different domains is often astonishingly similar: to bring order to experience, to make something that will endure after one's death, to do something that allows humankind to go beyond its present powers, are very common themes."[317]

COSMIC CHOREOGRAPHY

One leader in the arts world who has leaned into a condition of awe while drawing together art and science is choreographer Dana Tai Soon Burgess, who has been described by *The Washington Post* as "not only a Washington prize, but a national dance treasure."[318] The eponymous Dana Tai Soon Burgess Dance Company (DTSBDC), founded to artistically convey "shared human experiences in the context of

316 Angela Anderson, "Art Draws Out the Beauty of Physics," *Symmetry*, April 12, 2016, accessed November 14, 2020.

317 Csikszentmihalyi, *Flow and the Psychology of Discovery and Invention*, 38.

318 Sarah Kaufman, "Burgess at 20: Dance Fully Evolved," *The Washington Post*, September 23, 2012, accessed August 24, 2020.

historical events and personal stories," is renowned as Washington, DC's premier modern dance company.[319]

On a wintry December evening in 2018, rows of dance enthusiasts—or space enthusiasts, or perhaps fans of both disciplines—warmed the auditorium of the Smithsonian National Portrait Gallery for a space race–inspired dance performance. The program I held in my hand promised the performance would be an exploration of "the connection between humanity and space, touching upon America's idealism around the space race, the mystery of the cosmos, and the fragility of life."[320]

In this particular work, entitled *We Choose to Go to the Moon*, the historical events the dance company was to feature were the Apollo lunar landings. Burgess had developed the piece in partnership with NASA several years earlier, and the Portrait Gallery opened its doors to the public that night for a series of encore performances to commemorate the fiftieth anniversary of Apollo 8, the first manned spacecraft to reach the Moon, orbit it, and safely return to Earth. Event-goers—including me—chatted among themselves or perused their printed concert programs as artists and scientists filtered into the venue and warmly greeted a man whose graceful ease, creative aura, and balletic posture suggested he was none other than Dana Tai Soon Burgess himself.

319 "About DTSBDC," Dana Tai Soon Burgess Dance Company, accessed November 14, 2020.

320 Dana Tai Soon Burgess Dance Company, *We Choose to Go to the Moon*, National Portrait Gallery, Washington, DC, December 18, 2018.

After a suspenseful wait, the evening began with a couple of short scientific lectures by planetary geologist Dr. James ("Jim") Zimbelman and spaceflight historian Dr. Teasel Muir-Harmony of the National Air and Space Museum. At last, the dancers emerged on stage, yet as the dancing commenced, the science education portion of the evening was far from over. As I was surprised to discover, Burgess had not simply created choreography set to 1960s pop songs inspired by the space exploration era. He had also chosen to set his dancers' movements to recorded speech, from President John F. Kennedy's speech at Rice University announcing the Apollo lunar expedition to interviews with scientists running those missions. The dance phrasing moved in perfect timing with the audio phrasing, with the performing artists repeating a signature series of movements to reinforce the tagline of the Rice University speech and the title of the dance performance as President Kennedy's voice boomed,

There is no strife, no prejudice, no national conflict in outer space as yet. Its hazards are hostile to us all. Its conquest deserves the best of all mankind, and its opportunity for peaceful cooperation may never come again. But why, some say, the Moon? Why choose this as our goal? And they may well ask, why climb the highest mountain? Why, thirty-five years ago, fly the Atlantic? ...

We choose to go to the Moon. We choose to go to the Moon in this decade and do the other things, not because they are easy, but because they are hard; because that goal will serve to organize and measure the best of our energies and skills, because that challenge is one that we are willing to accept, one we are unwilling to postpone, and one we intend to win, and the others, too.[321]

"But why the Moon?" was a question more than one audience member probably would have liked to ask Burgess. A post-performance panel with the choreographer and guest lecturers revealed that the idea of a collaboration between the DTSBDC and NASA was itself sparked by a chance encounter on a trip skyward. As Burgess and his husband, Jameson Freeman, were boarding a flight from Washington, DC, to Santa Fe, New Mexico, in late 2013—for one of many frequent trips to visit Burgess's ailing father—he placed a stuffed Elroy doll in the seat next to him and began photographing it. Such things are, Burgess joked to the audience, "apparently what artists do for fun."[322]

Who, you may ask, is Elroy? Freeman detailed on his blog, "Dana somehow acquired a small, stuffed 'Elroy' character (from [the 1960s space-themed] *The Jetsons* cartoon series) and found it funny to bring him with us to photograph at various locations—from [the] airport bar to [the] yoga studio. … The first leg of our westward trip was to Houston from DC, and the third seat in our row was empty … so Elroy was sitting in it, with [the] seatbelt fastened."[323]

As Burgess was photographing the doll—he recounted to us—he looked up to find a woman standing in the aisle who announced in good humor upon recognizing the

---

321 John F. Kennedy, "We Choose to Go to the Moon," Rice University, Houston, Texas, September 12, 1962.

322 Dana Tai Soon Burgess Dance Company, *We Choose to Go to the Moon.*

323 Jameson Freeman, "Serendipity," Self-Center (blog), December 14, 2018.

space-themed character, "I believe Elroy is in my seat!" Burgess apologized. "That's alright," said his fellow passenger, as she fetched a NASA button from her bag and pinned it onto the doll. Once settled into their seats, the two travelers turned to each other and asked with great curiosity, "What kind of work do you do?" Burgess's seatmate turned out to be none other than a high-ranking NASA official: Barbara Zelon, the communications manager for the Orion Spacecraft program. A riveting discussion of the arts and the mystery of the cosmos ensued.[324]

"We talked most of the flight—about dance (both her daughters danced and one is a choreographer in New York) and space (of course), and as we debarked, I invited her (and her daughters) to come to see Dana's dance company at the Kennedy Center in a few months' time," Freeman recounted on his blog.[325]

As Burgess gazed into the night sky from the porch of his parent's home in Santa Fe, his conversation with Zelon remained fresh in his mind.

"All my projects have a personal interest factor," Burgess said of his creative process. "Something occurs in my life and I think, 'This is fascinating—I need to learn more.'"[326]

---

324 Dana Tai Soon Burgess Dance Company, *We Choose to Go to the Moon.*
325 Freeman, "Serendipity."
326 Victoria Dawson, "A Dancer and a Scientist Deliver a New Take on the Moon Walk," *Smithsonian Magazine*, September 14, 2015, accessed August 24, 2020.

Particularly in the context of his father's declining health, the question of the human relationship to the heavens came into sharp relief.

"We've all looked up into the night sky at one point and pondered existence," Burgess said. "What does that mean in terms of our own human experience?"[327]

As Burgess let his own thoughts wander skyward, a constellation of artistic possibilities began to crystallize in his imagination: "I started realizing what our shared relationship to the sky is all the way around the world and how we have so many stories and different ways that we understand and justify what the cosmos means to each individual."[328]

Thus, Burgess resolved to dedicate his next dance project to "people's relationship to space, the mystery of the cosmos, and the fragility of life." Burgess contacted Zelon about his idea, and the seeds for his collaboration with NASA were planted.[329]

"She totally understood it because so much of what NASA is trying to do is disperse available information about the theories and concepts discovered about space," the choreographer recounted. "[NASA] is always interested in disseminating

327 Emily Codik, "Dana Tai Soon Burgess Premieres Fluency in Four in Tribute to His Late Father," *Washingtonian*, September 11, 2015, accessed August 24, 2020.

328 Jane O'Brien, "NASA Collaborates on Interpretive Dance about Space," BBC, October 7, 2015, accessed November 24, 2020.

329 James S. Kim, "Over the Moon with Dana Tai Soon Burgess," *Character Media*, August 29, 2015, accessed August 24, 2020.

information through traditional ways and non-traditional methods such as art."[330]

Burgess started his new dance project by interviewing multiple past and present NASA employees, including a former astronaut, a senior technologist in high-energy astrophysics, and a physicist working in gamma-ray astronomy, as well as a medicine woman from Santa Fe whose father was an electrician for the Apollo missions. Freeman praised Zelon for being "instrumental in making the NASA connections that helped supply the dance with incredible space imagery, as well as the introductions for some of the interviews that were featured in the sound score."[331]

Burgess also sought to contact scientists at the National Air and Space Museum. Yet in the museum world, the choreographer's email was shuffled from one person's inbox to another while he waited for a response. At last, Zimbelman, a planetary geologist who had worked for twenty years at the National Air and Space Museum, seized the out-of-the-box opportunity to connect with Burgess, thinking, *Dance company? Sure! I'll see why he wants to talk to a scientist.*[332]

Originally, Burgess's conversations were intended as research to lay the groundwork for portraying multiple personal stories through dance.

330 Ibid.
331 Freeman, "Serendipity."
332 Dawson, "A Dancer and a Scientist Deliver a New Take on the Moon Walk."

"I didn't want this to be a sort of college lecture," he decided. "We need something on a human level that we can access because these stories and folks are the ones that we're all fascinated by."[333]

Yet the more Burgess talked with the scientists, the more he became convinced their stories should be directly incorporated into the soundtrack.

"There was a passion and wisdom about their voices that I loved," Burgess said of the scientists. "And their voices were so diverse—they sounded like music to me."[334]

The final product was therefore a dance performance set to a mixed soundtrack incorporating excerpts of President Kennedy's speech, interviews with astronauts and scientists, magnetic pulses of planets, an indigenous archaeologist's narration of the Comanche Nation's spiritual beliefs about celestial bodies beyond the Earth, and 1960s pop songs.

"It has all these different vignettes that then sort of lead the audience through, not just scientific information, but through nostalgia, through different perspectives of what the cosmos means to them and then arrives at this place where, essentially, we make it to the Moon and we look back at Earth," Burgess explained.[335]

---

333   Kim, "Over the Moon with Dana Tai Soon Burgess."

334   Dawson, "A Dancer and a Scientist Deliver a New Take on the Moon Walk."

335   Sydney Lee, "Professor Brings the Space Race to the Stage in Dance Show at the National Portrait Gallery," *The GW Hatchet*, December 15, 2018, accessed August 29, 2020.

While working on the project, Burgess gained a deep appreciation for parallels in the processes of scientific and artistic discovery.

"There's a creative process that's built in through research to discovery, which is the same as what a choreographer uses," said Burgess. "They research a subject, they work in their laboratory—which is the dance studio—on movement that will convey that, and they have this performance."[336]

Burgess elaborated in an interview with *Smithsonian Magazine*, "Like a choreographer, a scientist cannot reach for discovery without leaps of faith—a hypothesis of what could be."[337]

As for Zimbelman, he expressed hope that the arts would become integrated into space exploration itself. "The space program could benefit from sending a poet to some of these places," he told the BBC. "Different ways of expressing the human emotion of space flight—that is missing, I think, and I hope Dana is the beginning of drawing the public in from that side."[338]

We Choose to Go to the Moon debuted in September 2015 at the John F. Kennedy Center for the Performing Arts, premiering alongside three other repertory works in an evening titled *Fluency in Four*. Burgess dedicated the work as "an ode" to his late father, Joseph James Burgess, Jr., who had passed away in November 2014, and the space pioneers of his father's

336 Ibid.
337 Dawson, "A Dancer and a Scientist Deliver a New Take on the Moon Walk."
338 O'Brien, "NASA Collaborates on Interpretive Dance about Space."

generation. The work's world premiere received significant media attention and favorable reviews in *The Washington Post* and several other publications, and the dance company went on to present the piece at NASA sites across the country.[339]

Less than a year later, the Smithsonian Institution appointed Burgess as the first-ever choreographer in residence, opening the door wide open for him to create new works inspired by museum exhibitions and further develop dance as an educational medium. The Portrait Gallery thus became a formal inspiration and venue for Burgess's dance projects.[340]

The company took to the Portrait Gallery stage on a cold December evening in 2018 for a reprised performance, which was the one I attended. Burgess dedicated that performance to another son of the space era—his father-in-law, who had recently passed away—just as he had commemorated his own father years before in the debut performance.[341]

THE CHRYSALIS PROJECT

Dr. Hannah Schneider, an American-born, Russian-raised and -trained orchestral conductor, found her opportunity to express and cultivate awe in fusing the media of dance, film, and classical music to present multiple interpretations of the theme "chrysalis."

339 Sarah L. Kaufman, "Dana Tai Soon Burgess Dancers Cosmically Intertwine Art and Science," *The Washington Post*, September 20, 2015, accessed October 13, 2019.

340 "Dana Tai Soon Burgess," Dana Tai Soon Burgess Dance Company, accessed November 14, 2020.

341 Dana Tai Soon Burgess Dance Company, *We Choose to Go to the Moon*.

Schneider's CHRYSALIS Project unites an orchestra, a film production company, and a team of composers and world-renowned dancers and choreographers to push the boundaries on how these three arts forms are integrated with each other. "Usually it is one that is the primary focus, and the others fall into place behind it," Schneider explained in a video interview. The CHRYSALIS Project seeks instead to use the "new digital [communications] frontier" of the pandemic to create together, from scratch, new works that place the integrated trio of these art forms front and center.[342]

I first met Schneider during a summer abroad in 2013, when she happened to be an undergraduate student at my alma mater, Georgetown University. Prior to Georgetown, she had studied violin performance at Moscow's Tchaikovsky Conservatory. In the years that followed, we overlapped from time to time in Washington, DC, where she updated me on the latest developments of her blossoming career: first recording a classical music album of young musicians in the North Caucasus; then becoming personal administrative assistant to Russian conductor Valery Gergiev, the artistic and general director of the Mariinsky Theatre in St. Petersburg; and eventually pursuing graduate studies at the University of Oxford as a Rhodes Scholar. While completing her doctorate in Soviet opera and also conducting the Oxford Philharmonic Orchestra, Schneider founded Oxford Alternative Orchestra, an ensemble dedicated to the intersection of classical music and social impact.

342 "Interview with Our Artistic Director," The CHRYSALIS Project, January 28, 2021, YouTube video, 4:47.

In 2019 and early 2020, Schneider had been traveling nearly continually, conducting professionally in the United Kingdom, the United States, Ukraine, and locations across Russia as far as eastern Siberia. Suddenly, the COVID-19 pandemic brought live, in-person concerts to a halt. It was "a dark time for artists around the world trying to figure out how to keep making a living," Schneider told me over the telephone in October 2020.

During this dark time of confinement, separated from her audiences and musicians, the awe-inspiring image of the chrysalis came to mind. "The chrysalis is that point in the butterfly's life cycle where it's in a cocoon; it's confined, constrained; it's in the dark; and it has to be there for a long time in order to become the glorious creature that it's going to be," Schneider explained in her video interview.[343]

She began formulating a project to do with the Oxford Alternative Orchestra that would be "worthwhile" for everyone and speak to essential questions: "If you don't have any hope, why not? If you have hope, where does it come from?" Schneider envisioned a more innovative initiative than a virtual concert, and she was clear she "didn't want just dark pieces of art that reflect the mess we are in." "I want hope; I want regeneration," Schneider affirmed, pointing to the chrysalis as the image in nature that inspired this idea.

The result was a series of choreographed, classically composed, professionally filmed videos. The collaborating artists had "a lot of license" and "few artistic parameters," but the

343 Ibid.

goal was to "end with images of hope and inspiration, and with light rather than darkness, color rather than blackness" that illustrate "coming out of constraint into freedom"—all of which, Schneider explained to me, "can be interpreted theoretically but also visually."

As Schneider wove a preview for me with her words, I felt transported to other landscapes, as though we were once again international travel companions exploring new settings and realities. She hinted at a Korean concept in which two classical dancers, dressed delicately in white, are juxtaposed with a contemporary avant-garde structure in Seoul. The soft, floating movements of the dancers contrast with the harsh brutalist architecture as they strive to create grace, beauty, and gentleness in an imposing and austere world. The Americas concept is set in two locations: a black box theater in New York that serves as a nest, and the ruins of Godstow Abbey, a twelfth-century Gothic structure in Oxford, England. The nest features two dancers, covered in feathers and fighting to find form and shape and emerge into life. The abbey, on the other hand, shows the musicians and open blue skies, which weave the tapestry in which the dancers can take flight.

By late January 2021, I received news that a part of my own life was about to grind to a halt. Suddenly, hope, regeneration, and the pursuit of meaning were top of mind for me. As I was spending a Saturday afternoon in a burst of frenetic activity, a friend reminded me that it was almost time for the CHRYSALIS Project's public debut.

Chrysalis: Burkina Faso, the first of a series of the CHRYS-ALIS Project's orchestral and dance performance videos, opened with the camera panning onto dance artist Aguibou Bougabali Sanou viewed from behind, with his torso curled up so his head was out of view. In its place, a few of his fingers waved above his shoulders. The sight of it made me laugh, not at him, but at myself. Have we not all, at least once in our lives, hoped for consciousness as beautiful and light as a butterfly in flight, only to realize that our current state of mind is more akin to the squirming of an inelegant caterpillar?

In the short film's less than five minutes of runtime, the precision of the classical musicians, the emotional depth of the accompanying Burkinabè vocalist, and the increasingly free and vibrant movements of the dancer settled down my caterpillar mind and reminded it how to become a butterfly.

***

We Choose to Go to the Moon and the CHRYSALIS Project are but two examples of how the sciences and the arts both arc toward a "condition of awe." When they are drawn together, they can create intellectually and aesthetically illuminating experiences that invite us to contemplate the mystery and majesty of the natural world and the cosmos and guide us toward hope, meaning, and interconnectedness.

PART IV:

OUR FUTURE IS INTERDISCIPLINARY

CHAPTER 10:

THE CASE FOR INTERDISCIPLINARITY

——

The inspiring stories in the previous chapters showcase the impactful outcomes of successful collaborations between science and art and make the case for interdisciplinarity. Multiple definitions for interdisciplinarity exist, but my usage of the term coheres with Wayne State University professor emeritus Dr. Moti Nissani's "minimalist" definition of interdisciplinarity as "bringing together distinctive components of two or more disciplines."[344] Within each story presented in this book, those "two or more disciplines" involved both a scientific discipline and an artistic discipline.

This collection of stories suggested to me that interdisciplinarity offers many potential advantages. These stories seemed to serve as compelling examples of how working at

---

344 Moti Nissani, "Fruits, Salads, and Smoothies: A Working Definition of Interdisciplinarity," *Journal of Educational Thought* 29 no. 2 (August 1995): 121–128.

the intersection of disciplines allows us to explore and contemplate our universe and transform and save lives.

I wondered if the advantages evidenced in these stories extended more broadly to interdisciplinary endeavors at large. However, I had hand-picked these stories precisely because of their status as success stories. Given this clear selection bias, I knew I could not make broad claims about the benefits of interdisciplinarity without doing more research.

As it turns out, the work of several researchers before me upholds the idea that seeking solutions at the intersection of disciplines may not only result in innovative breakthroughs, but may also hold other advantages.

"Great discoveries and shifts in conventional thinking have been traditionally attributed to researchers crossing disciplinary boundaries," Denise Caruso and Dr. Diana Rhoten wrote in a 2001 white paper on interdisciplinarity in "The Age of Information."[345]

In her book *Creating Interdisciplinary Campus Cultures: A Model for Strength and Sustainability*, Dr. Julie Thompson Klein noted that "interdisciplinarity is associated with bold advances in knowledge, solutions to urgent social problems, an edge in technological innovation, and a more integrative educational experience."[346]

---

345 Denise Caruso and Diana Rhoten, "Lead, Follow, Get Out of the Way: Sidestepping the Barriers to Effective Practice of Interdisciplinarity" (The Hybrid Vigor Institute, 2011), 6.

346 Julie Thompson Klein, *Creating Interdisciplinary Campus Cultures: A Model for Strength and Sustainability* (San Francisco: John Wiley & Sons, 2009), 2.

Furthermore, multiple peer-reviewed academic articles and scientifically validated studies provide compelling evidence that the stories featured in this book are more than simple anecdotes.

The following are a few of the advantages of interdisciplinarity that surfaced in these stories and are supported by peer-reviewed research findings.

IT LEADS TO BREAKTHROUGHS IN INNOVATION.

Several studies suggest that significant and creative advancements are made at interdisciplinary intersections.

Drs. Ling Jian, Brent Clark, and Daniel Turban found that "interdisciplinary idea networking"—or more simply put, regularly seeking knowledge from other domains or disciplines—can lead to "more breakthrough inventions."[347]

Drs. Cornelius Herstatt and Katharina Kalogerakis's research in new product development found that "analogies can trigger breakthrough ideas" when "problem solutions" are transferred "from one industry or domain to another."[348]

---

347 Lin Jiang et al. "Creating Breakthroughs: The Role of Interdisciplinary Idea Networking and Organizational Contexts," *Academy of Management Proceedings* no. 1 (2015): 18645.

348 Cornelius Herstatt and Katharina Kalogerakis, "How to Use Analogies for Breakthrough Innovations," *International Journal of Innovation and Technology Management* 2 no. 3 (2005): 331–347.

IT FOSTERS BETTER, MORE INCLUSIVE LEARNING IN ACADEMIC SETTINGS.

Research shows that interdisciplinary learning is more enjoyable, effective, collaborative, and inclusive.

Multiple peer-reviewed studies suggest that interdisciplinary curricular programs increase students' satisfaction and self-confidence and reduce anxiety in secondary and post-secondary educational settings.[349, 350, 351]

Education scholar Dr. Sheena Ghanbari, in a 2015 study on learning across disciplines, argued that "visual and performing arts have the ability to enhance learning in other subjects." Noting that "arts coursework is inquiry-based, which means it revolves around questioning and understanding concepts versus finding the answer to a given problem," she pointed to other studies showing that an "inquiry-based model of learning is analogous with principles of critical thinking" that higher education is intended to develop. Ghanbari also noted that incorporating artistic inquiry into STEM education appeals to varied learning styles, including visual, auditory, and kinesthetic.[352]

---

349 Filippos Filippou et al., "Interdisciplinary Greek Traditional Dance Course: Impact on Student Satisfaction and Anxiety," *International Journal of Instruction* 11 no. 3 (2018): 363–374.

350 Barbara M. Olds and Ronald L. Miller, "The Effect of a First-Year Integrated Engineering Curriculum on Graduation Rates and Student Satisfaction: A Longitudinal Study," *Journal of Engineering Education* 93 no. 1 (2004): 25–35.

351 Nasra N. Ayuob et al., "Interdisciplinary Integration of the CVS Module and Its Effect on Faculty and Student Satisfaction as Well as Student Performance," *BMC Medical Education* 12 no. 50 (2012).

352 Sheena Ghanbari, "Learning Across Disciplines: A Collective Case Study of Two University Programs That Integrate the Arts with STEM," *International Journal of Education and the Arts* 16 no. 7 (2015).

Ghanbari's case study of two university programs found that their integration of the arts with STEM education yielded enhanced collaboration, retention of material, and enjoyment of learning.[353] Similarly, students who participated in multidisciplinary project-based learning at the Massachusetts Institute of Technology (MIT) reported significant improvements in their ability to work in teams and solve complex problems.[354]

Interdisciplinary programs may also lead to more balanced gender representation in STEM fields. In 1987, the University of Rhode Island launched an International Engineering Program, in which students earn dual degrees in engineering and a foreign language. This program not only fulfilled its intended purpose of growing the university's once-waning foreign language and literature programs but also yielded an unanticipated benefit: women "enrolled in engineering in increasing numbers" while the "academic quality" of the university's engineering students "improved."[355]

Drs. Hannah Stewart-Gambino and Jenn Stroud Rossman pointed to multiple recent examples of "integrated, contextualized learning that appear to be effective in recruiting women and other underrepresented populations," questioning why it was ever deemed necessary to "'strip out' the

353 Ibid.
354 Rafael L. Bras et al., "Students' Perceptions of Terrascope, A Project-Based Freshman Learning Community," *Journal of Science Education and Technology* 16 no. 4 (2007): 349–364.
355 Karin Fischer, "In Rhode Island, an Unusual Marriage of Engineering and Languages Lures Students," *The Chronicle*, May 18, 2012, accessed March 8, 2021.

historical and societal contexts" from STEM education content in the first place.[356]

IT BREAKS US OUT OF A ZERO-SUM GAME.

Especially in recent decades, the arts and the sciences have been painted as two divergent forces locked in a competition for resources.

Higher education in particular is seen, in the words of Stewart-Gambino and Rossman, as "perennially caught in the tension of a dual mission—providing society with a technically and scientifically literate workforce and a citizenry with the analytical perspectives gained from the traditional liberal arts, particularly humanities and the arts."[357] In a 2015 *New York Times* opinion piece entitled "What Is the Point of College?" philosopher and cultural theorist Dr. Kwame Anthony Appiah characterized this tension as "the choice between 'utility' and 'utopia.'"[358]

Stewart-Gambino and Rossman noted that multiple developments, including a steeper "educational pathway to socioeconomic security," are fundamentally changing "the meaning and content of what an educated citizenry knows or ought to know, and the result is an embattled liberal arts, humanities,

356 Hannah Stewart-Gambino and Jenn Stroud Rossman, "Often Asserted, Rarely Measured: The Value of Integrating Humanities, STEM, and Arts in Undergraduate Learning," The National Academies of Sciences, Engineering, and Medicine (2015).

357 Ibid.

358 Kwame Anthony Appiah, "What Is the Point of College?" *The New York Times Magazine*, September 13, 2015, accessed March 8, 2021.

and arts community fighting to defend their relevance and value to an increasingly skeptical public."[359]

Data from the National Center for Education Statistics indicate that, between 2011 and 2017, the number of degrees awarded annually in the United States in almost every subject in the humanities and social sciences decreased by more than 10 percent, while the number of degrees awarded in all STEM subjects increased.[360]

Meanwhile, humanities programs have been dwindling because of budget cuts prompted by the global financial crisis in 2008.[361] Universities and colleges across the United States have "taken steps to reduce or cut arts and humanities programs, faculty positions, or institutions on campuses" by eliminating undergraduate and graduate programs of study and closing whole departments or collapsing them into one.[362]

"Humanities programs are closing every year, and if that trend continues, the liberal art disciplines might even cease to exist as mainstream academic programs," computer scientist Dr. Lior Shamir warned in early 2020.[363]

359 Stewart-Gambino and Rossman, "Often Asserted, Rarely Measured: The Value of Integrating Humanities, STEM, and Arts in Undergraduate Learning," 2.
360 Rick Mullin, "Behind the Scenes at the STEM–Humanities Culture War," *Chemical & Engineering News* 97 no. 29 (July 16, 2019).
361 Ibid.
362 "Colleges Facing Cuts to Arts and Humanities Programs," College Art Association of America, November 8, 2018, accessed March 10, 2021.
363 Lior Shamir, "A Case Against the STEM Rush," *Inside Higher Ed*, February 3, 2020, accessed March 10, 2021.

There are few hard metrics to indicate the impact of a dearth of art and humanities on students' educational outcomes and employability.[364] However, faculty and higher education administrators have expressed concerns about reduced exposure to the humanities and the trend toward increased specialization.

"A lot of major institutions are requiring more credits within majors, restricting the time for outside courses. They are increasing the number of courses you need to take to complete those degrees, and it's a zero-sum game," said Dr. Charles Blaich, director of the Center of Inquiry and the Higher Education Data Sharing Consortium at Wabash College.[365]

However, interdisciplinary programs and projects have the potential to break us out of that zero-sum game. The stories in previous chapters offer examples of such scenarios. For example, the arts can be combined with science and technology in makerspaces to develop products or launch projects with educational, health-related, or otherwise societally beneficial components. The arts can be integrated into medical training, practice, and research to benefit both patients and care providers. Performing artists and scientific researchers can collaborate with each other to enhance scientific research and communication of findings to larger audiences while creating art in the process.

---

364 Mullin, "Behind the Scenes at the STEM–Humanities Culture War."
365 Ibid.

In order for us to break out of the zero-sum game by engaging in these types of interactions and collaborations across disciplinary boundaries, though, we must allow these disciplines to thrive in their own right. Sometimes artists will need the freedom simply to create art, and scientists will need the freedom simply to investigate science—and to do so, they will both need sufficient space, recognition, and resources to support them.

IT HELPS US STAY RELEVANT TO THE FUTURE OF WORK IN THE AGE OF ARTIFICIAL INTELLIGENCE.

Interdisciplinary thinking is the key to surviving the future of work.

An interdisciplinary team of researchers at the University of Cambridge drawn from the fields of anthropology, design research, and strategic policy argued in a technical report published in 2009 that interdisciplinary innovation is essential to an economy that is based more heavily on intellectual capital than on material production:

"In the knowledge economy, it is often the case that the right knowledge to solve a problem is in a different place to the problem itself, so interdisciplinary innovation is an essential tool for the future. There are also many problems today that need more than one kind of knowledge to solve them, so interdisciplinary innovation is also an essential tool for the challenging problems of today."[366]

---

366 Alan F. Blackwell et al., *Radical Innovation: Crossing Knowledge Boundaries with Interdisciplinary Teams* (Cambridge: University of Cambridge Computer Laboratory, 2009), 3.

By 2025, nearly 50 percent of work tasks will be done by machines, according to the World Economic Forum's report *The Future of Jobs 2020*. The transition to automation is expected to "displace" eighty-five million jobs by that time. Fortunately, it will also create an estimated ninety-seven million new jobs.[367] The future holds new opportunities—but they will look little like what preceded them.

Such projections identify areas of opportunity in STEM fields. According to the World Economic Forum's projection, most jobs will exist in healthcare, artificial intelligence, biotechnology, robotics, software engineering, and digital product management.[368] Thus, the future of work is in STEM.

Meanwhile, information and data processing, administrative tasks, and routine manual jobs are increasingly being handed over to machines.[369] As technology advances exponentially, we will need to tap into what makes us human: the ability to seek understanding of and empathize with others, to aestheticize and metaphorize, and to make value judgments. Thus, the future of work is in the arts and humanities.

It is skills from both the science and the arts that will keep us relevant to the future of work in a post-digital era. Thus, interdisciplinarity is not only a key to innovation but also a key to survival. David Epstein presented a series of arguments in his book *Range: Why Generalists Triumph in a Specialized World* that uphold this conclusion. In his discussion

---

367 "The Future of Jobs 2020," World Economic Forum, October 20, 2020.
368 Ibid.
369 Ibid.

of the advantages generalists have over specialists, Epstein referred to "kind" versus "wicked" domains, a distinction first made by psychologist Dr. Robin Hogarth.[370]

In kind domains, "patterns repeat over and over, and feedback is extremely accurate and usually very rapid." Pattern recognition, Epstein noted, is relatively easy to automate.[371] Working in kind domains is where machines have the advantage over humans.

In "wicked domains," on the other hand, "the rules of the game are often unclear or incomplete, there may or may not be repetitive patterns and they may not be obvious, and feedback is often delayed, inaccurate, or both."[372] Solving "wicked" problems is where humans have the advantage over machines.

If work involving simple, repetitive tasks is to become the principal territory of our robot colleagues, then we humans should do all we can to become very good at what is left to us: solving big-picture problems amid complexity and ambiguity.

How, then, do humans become good at solving wicked-domain problems?

Hyperspecialization, perhaps surprisingly, is not the answer; it is good for kind domains but not for wicked domains. "When narrow specialization is combined with an unkind

---

370 Epstein, *Range: Why Generalists Triumph in a Specialized World*, 20–21.
371 Ibid.
372 Ibid.

domain, the human tendency to rely on experience of familiar patterns can backfire horribly," Epstein warned.[373] This phenomenon, which organizational psychologist and Rice University professor Dr. Erik Dane coined "cognitive entrenchment," is precisely what the future workforce ought to avoid.[374]

Instead, what helps create breakthroughs in solving "wicked" problems is analogical thinking, which by definition involves breaking out of a single frame of reference. In other words, the key is to "vary challenges within a domain drastically, and, as a fellow researcher put it, insist on 'having one foot outside of your world,'" Dane proposed.[375]

In addition to developing the analogical thinking that is critical to work in the age of automation, interdisciplinarity is also essential to developing a workforce filled with "T-shaped" people, a term used to describe individuals with the depth of skill to make substantial contributions in one domain and the breadth of general knowledge to collaborate across multiple other domains.

Dr. I. F. Oskam's research yielded the conclusion that a "well-prepared engineering workforce" must include "T-shaped" engineers—i.e., engineers with "in-depth knowledge of one discipline and a broad knowledge base in adjacent areas or in general business or entrepreneurial fields"—to

---

373 Ibid.
374 Ibid.
375 Ibid.

meet the global demand for interdisciplinary innovation within their field of practice.[376]

The National Science Foundation (NSF), an independent US Government agency that supports science and engineering research and innovation, has explicitly acknowledged, in announcing its mission to prepare for the "future of work at the human-technology frontier," that the technicians of the future "are cross-disciplinary workers, immersed in diverse platforms and interrelated systems that once belonged to single industry sectors."[377]

Furthermore, McKinsey & Company, a top management consulting firm, revealed in a January 2019 report on closing the future-skills gap, that digitization and automation were creating a demand for new skill sets that would require 25 percent of the global workforce to significantly broaden their cross-disciplinary skills along with their technological skills by 2020.[378]

***

As the stories I curated suggest and research shows, interdisciplinarity can catalyze innovation, improve learning, reduce competition for resources, and equip the labor force

376 I. F. Oskam, "T-Shaped Engineers for Interdisciplinary Innovation: An Attractive Perspective for Young People as Well as a Must for Innovative Organisations," *37th Annual Conference—Attracting Students in Engineering*, Rotterdam, The Netherlands, vol. 14 (2009): 1–10.

377 Preparing Technicians for the Future of Work, National Science Foundation, accessed November 14, 2020.

378 Viktor Hediger et al., "Closing the Future-Skills Gap," McKinsey, January 29, 2019, accessed September 24, 2020.

to participate in a rapidly changing economic and technological landscape.

CHAPTER 11:

EIGHT PRINCIPLES OF INTERDISCIPLINARY INNOVATION

———

During the writing process, I discovered that the purpose of this book is not simply to tell interesting stories about cross-disciplinary innovations. This book is, more importantly, an exploration of how we can encourage more such innovations to take place.

When I first set out to write this book, I did not expect to uncover principles for innovating, nor did I intend to examine the components involved in major breakthroughs. It seemed to me that there were already plenty of well-established thought leaders on those topics.

My intention was primarily to indulge my intellectual curiosity by bringing into conversation multiple disciplines that interested me and set to paper what I discovered. My highest ambition was nothing more than to crystallize and organize my own thoughts and then do the small favor of sharing them with others who might find them interesting or useful.

As I delved into the process of researching and writing, though, common threads emerged from the collection of stories I was gathering that I could not ignore. What surfaced in many of these stories about impactful interdisciplinary collaborations were noteworthy ways in which the people involved approached their work—what were, it seemed, good practices for keeping the circumstances favorable for successful innovation.

These are the lessons I distilled from patterns that emerged in these stories:

1. ASSUME THAT EVERYTHING COULD BE RELEVANT.

While writing this book, I noticed innovations at the intersection of STEM and the arts coming from people who were experts in their fields and whose power stemmed not solely from sustained attention to their areas of expertise but also from their willingness to view anything and everything as potentially relevant to their work, and to view anyone and everyone as a potential partner in that work.

Specialists are trained to know the boundaries of their disciplines. However, what is relevant to one's discipline is not necessarily limited to just that particular discipline. While the subject matter and terminology of a given discipline are distinct from those of another, methodologies can be borrowed and adapted across disciplines.

Embracing this open attitude is what can take us from being completely stumped to utterly inspired. Remember Archimedes's quintessential eureka moment? As legend has it, the ancient Greek intellectual, charged with determining whether a votive crown was made of pure gold or a silver alloy, realized when he saw the water level rise as he entered the bathtub that the same effect could help him calculate the density of the crown. The veracity of this story is disputed.[379] However, whether the details of Archimedes's story are fact or fiction, it is thanks to this attitude—that anything might be relevant to solving the problem at hand—that plenty of other great discoveries have been made.

If a nineteenth-century logician had not been open to the possibility that philosophy could be relevant to algebra, binary code might not have been created and I might be stuck typing up these words on a typewriter instead of a computer.[380]

Because a modern-day choreographer was open to the possibility that NASA's work might somehow be relevant to the performing arts, he not only created a critically acclaimed dance performance but eventually became the first choreographer in residence of the world's largest museum and research complex.

Because a pair of Bolivian pediatric cardiologists were able to acknowledge that artisanal weaving might have something

379 David Biello, "Fact or Fiction?: Archimedes Coined the Term 'Eureka!' in the Bath," *Scientific American*, December 8, 2006, accessed March 5, 2021.
380 Epstein, *Range: Why Generalists Triumph in a Specialized World*, 33–34.

in common with constructing medical devices, they found a lifesaving technique literally in the hands of their patients' own family members.

The habit of constantly scanning the horizon for inspiration seems to be a hallmark of people who demonstrate a high level of creativity. "Creative individuals are remarkable for their ability to adapt to almost any situation and to make do with whatever is at hand to reach their goals," psychologist Dr. Mihaly Csikszentmihalyi noted in *Creativity: Flow and the Psychology of Discovery and Invention*.[381]

The ability to have this type of cross-contextual eureka moment is not necessarily rooted in a gift of innate creativity. Rather, it can be cultivated through a particular approach to problem-solving: launching what Csikszentmihalyi and Dr. Jacob Getzels have called "a period of rambling discovery."[382] A study by the two researchers demonstrated that "a period of rambling discovery at the start of a creatively minded project," in contrast to "premature closure," not only generates a larger volume of options to work with but also increases "the possibility of being exposed to influences that at first appear to be completely unrelated to the work at hand."[383]

Denise Shekerjian, the author of *Uncommon Genius: How Great Ideas Are Born*, has made a similar point: "What blocks a creative solution to a problem is often an overly narrow and

---

381 Csikszentmihalyi, *Creativity: Flow and the Psychology of Discovery and Invention*, 51.

382 Shekerjian, *Uncommon Genius: How Great Ideas Are Born*, 39.

383 Ibid.

single-minded concentration from a single frame of reference. The person who can combine frames of reference and draw connections between ostensibly unrelated points of view is likely to be the one who makes the creative breakthrough."[384]

By suspending assumptions about what is relevant and what is not, scientists, artists, and other innovators free themselves to make unexpected discoveries: origami is important for aerospace engineering, artisanal weaving can save the lives of children with heart defects, a choreographer can teach the public a great deal about the moon landing—and more.

2. ENGAGE WITH TOPICS YOU KNOW LITTLE ABOUT.

What is striking in so many of the stories I have curated about interdisciplinary innovations is that they emerged from bold and unexpected conversations between specialists in very different fields. I consider the willingness to engage with topics thoroughly outside one's field of expertise distinct from the willingness to suspend judgment about what might be relevant to one's work.

For example, I was particularly struck by the story behind the Barkin/Selissen Project's modern dance piece *Differential Cohomology*. Not every dance artist, when strolling through Central Park with a mathematician, would have the curiosity or courage to engage in a meaningful conversation about a complex theoretical concept at the cutting edge of the discipline—and not every mathematician would embrace the opportunity to take an active part in shaping the creative

---

384 Ibid.

vision to bring that concept onto the stage. Yet it is exactly that scenario that led to the making of a dance performed in both artistic and educational venues.

Innovators get out of their silos to pursue conversations with people in other fields while maintaining a real openness to active listening. Instead of saying "I don't know anything about that" and simply shutting down, they say, "Tell me more about that." They cultivate their curiosity and do not worry about appearing to be an expert on everything. Such conversations require the willingness to ask a question, and upon receiving an answer, the willingness to ask a follow-up question—and so forth.

Engaging in such conversations sounds straightforward enough in theory, but in practice, it requires reaching into one's reserves of humility. The deeper one goes into conversation with an expert in a different field, the more unfamiliar terminology and concepts are likely to come up. Actively engaging with a specialist in a different area of expertise inevitably means revealing the limits of one's knowledge about their field, which is hard and humbling. It is one thing to know and accept that you are not well-versed in someone else's field, yet another thing to openly admit that your knowledge of their field is limited, and something else altogether to lay bare the extent to which it is unfamiliar to you. It takes courage to ask questions that run the risk of showing what you do not know.

Moreover, specialists in different fields might fall into the awkward trap of presumed familiarity and use what they think is shared terminology, only to discover that a term they both use refers to entirely distinct concepts in their respective fields. For example, oceanographer Dr. Anand Gnanadesikan pointed out to me the pitfalls of the term "alpha," which has a very different meaning to physicists than it does to statisticians. Similarly, Dr. Perry Skeath, an electrical engineer who pivoted into integrative medicine research, told me specialists in different disciplines "do not even speak the same language" and "do not think in the same conceptual ways." In the end, the only way to get around this obstacle is to learn how to speak a little bit of that other conceptual language and wade through confusion together until you reach understanding, which requires the willingness to look somewhat foolish temporarily.

There is, however, an upside to engaging with someone far outside of one's field. It may be less intimidating than it seems for one simple reason: freedom from expectation. When you talk to someone who is specialized in a discipline that is adjacent to yours, there is an expectation that you will have some overlap in subject matter expertise, conceptual frameworks, and terminology, but it may be unclear where that overlap starts and ends. In that sense, it is somewhat risky; one moment you may find yourself walking on solid ground together, and the very next you may find yourself sinking into the quicksand of confusion (perhaps when you realize "alpha" does not mean what you think it means!). In contrast, when you enter a discussion with someone whose focus is in a discipline fundamentally distinct from your own, there is no assumption of overlapping knowledge. You are completely free to explore the treasure trove of each other's minds without the pressure to maintain the pretense that you have any knowledge about what they are telling you.

Letting go of the temptation to maintain appearances, and diving in with the fresh enthusiasm of a novice, is a key part of interdisciplinary engagement. As the authors of "Ten Simple Rules for a Successful Cross-Disciplinary Collaboration" wrote, "Make the most of being a novice. No one expects you to know everything about the new field. In particular, there is no pressure to understand everything immediately, so ask the 'stupid' questions. Demonstrating your interest and enthusiasm is of much higher value than pretending to know everything already."[385]

Shekerjian would concur. "Cut short the floundering and you've cut short the possible creative outcomes. Cheat on the stumbling-about, and you've robbed yourself of the raw stuff that feeds the imagination," she wrote.[386]

No one person can be a bona fide expert in everything, but we can all find connections. These connections may take us in directions we never would have imagined previously if we ask thoughtful questions of others, actively listen to their answers, and remain open to all kinds of possibilities.

3. CHANGE YOUR ENVIRONMENT.

"It is easier to enhance creativity by changing conditions in the environment than by trying to make people think more

---

385 Bernhard Knapp et al., "Ten Simple Rules for a Successful Cross-Disciplinary Collaboration," *PLOS Computational Biology* 11 no. 4 (April 30, 2015): e1004214.

386 Shekerjian, *Uncommon Genius: How Great Ideas Are Born*, 32–33.

creatively," Csikszentmihalyi asserted in *Creativity: Flow and the Discovery of Psychology and Invention*.[387]

One of the simplest ways to change "conditions in the environment" is to bring new people into it. A way to do so is to facilitate encounters among people who should be meeting but are not.

For example, when Julia Kaganskiy convened the ArtsTech meetups in New York, many people working at the cross-section of arts and technology in New York for years had never met one another, because they had been siloed in their own industry sectors. They had not seen a reason to seek each other out until Kaganskiy invited them to encounter one another and provided the forum for doing so. These meetups led to interesting collaborations that had innovative outcomes, such as the world's first digital auction, and all sorts of art business arose out of the arts and technology incubator she launched.

Another way to change your environment is to move out of it and step into another one. For example, Princeton's "Flock Logic" project arose after choreographer Susan Marshall attended Dr. Naomi Leonard's scientific talk on flocking behavior in animals.

---

387 Csikszentmihalyi, *Creativity: Flow and the Discovery of Psychology and Invention*, 1.

4. WATCH HOW PEOPLE ARE SOLVING PROBLEMS THAT YOU ARE NOT TRYING TO SOLVE.

It might seem counterintuitive to watch how people are solving problems you are not trying to solve. Shouldn't you direct your energy and attention toward the problems you *are* trying to solve, you might ask? Yet many examples of innovations featured in this book arose when innovators paid attention to how people were solving problems that had nothing to do with—or so they thought—the problems that were on their mind.

Entrepreneur Mick Ebeling took note when he saw concert attendees standing right next to the music speakers. At first glance, it was not clear what was driving their behavior. When he realized these concertgoers were deaf, he understood they were trying to solve the problem of how to improve their perception of music through means other than hearing. Ebeling himself had not, in that moment, been thinking about how to create a better live music experience through non-auditory means. As a hearing individual, he was not concerned with how to feel the vibrations of the music himself; his eardrums and the rest of his auditory system were taking care of that for him just fine. Yet he was devoted in his career to creating new possibilities for individuals with disabilities, so what he saw was interesting and relevant to him, and he kept it in his mind after he left the concert.

In the case of Drs. Franz Freudenthal and Alexandra Heath, as they were agonizing over how to keep young Bolivian children with heart defects alive and healthy, these children's mothers and their *comadres* were using the time-tested techniques of Bolivian weaving traditions to create textiles. On the surface, these seemed to be two distinct and unrelated problems: how to heal sick children's hearts on the one hand and how to make useful goods on the other hand. On a technical level, though, the doctors were trying to solve a problem indigenous Bolivians had found the key to centuries ago: how to create a strong, flexible structure using a thin, breakable material. For Bolivian artisans, the structure was a textile good, and the material was thread; for the cardiologists, the structure was a heart device, and the material was a metal filament—but the underlying solution was surprisingly transferable.

5. RETAIN THE PLAYFULNESS OF CHILDHOOD.

In *Uncommon Genius: How Great Ideas Are Born*, Shekerjian identified play as a key component of encouraging creative "luck," quoting the words of psychologist Dr. Edward de Bono:

"If the purpose of chance in generating new ideas is to provide one with something to look at which one would not have looked for, then there may be methods of encouraging this process. Play is probably the ideal method. It must, however, be purposeless play without design and direction. Just as a carefully designed experiment is an attempt to hurry along the path of logical investigation, so play is an attempt to encourage the chance appearance of phenomena which would not be sought out. Playing around is an experiment with chance."[388]

---

388 Shekerjian, *Uncommon Genius: How Great Ideas Are Born*, 156–157.

According to de Bono, children stop playing when "the world changes from an unknown place in which wonderful things can happen into a familiar place in which there is an adequate explanation for everything." In contrast, Shekerjian noted, "[in] a quizzical, curious mind that notices the nuances and discrepancies, adequate explanations are too thin to suffice and tinkering with the possibilities becomes an enticing proposition. To retain the simple playfulness of childhood through one's riper years is what opens a person up to the creative possibilities within a situation. Amusing oneself is an effective way of encouraging that good fortune."[389]

Jordan Gray, the co-founder and managing director of CODAME ART+TECH, has acknowledged the value of play at the nexus of art and technology. Gray told the virtual attendees of an August 2020 Stanford University Leonardo Art Science Evening Rendezvous (LASER), "Play is core to everything we do. It's so important, and that's how we make space for innovation and everything else. And that is where creativity comes from: just being willing to play, being willing to make mistakes, and being willing to explore."[390]

Indulging in a playful moment can also serve as the conversation-opener that leads to a fruitful interdisciplinary collaboration. A prime example is the initial conversation between Dana Tai Soon Burgess, a choreographer, and Barbara Zelon, a NASA official, that sparked the idea for the space exploration–themed dance performance *We Choose to Go to the Moon*. That interaction started when Zelon pinned a NASA

389 Ibid.
390 "New Paradigms and Spaces for Artistic Expression."

button onto a plush character from *The Jetsons* Burgess was photographing playfully.

6. WORK IN DIVERSE TEAMS AND CROSS-CULTURAL SETTINGS.

A 2013 *Harvard Business Review* study entitled "How Diversity Can Drive Innovation" found "compelling evidence that diversity unlocks innovation and drives market growth." The study consisted of a "nationally representative survey of eighteen hundred professionals, forty case studies, and numerous focus groups and interviews" that examined both inherent diversity (traits one is born with) and acquired diversity (traits one gains from experience). Employees of companies whose leaders exhibited at least three inherent and three acquired diversity traits were 45 percent more likely to report a growth in market share over the previous year and 70 percent more likely to report that the firm had captured a new market than were their counterparts in firms whose leadership lacked such diversity.[391]

A study published in *Research Policy*, an academic journal that focuses on the policy, management, and economic studies of science, technology, and innovation, found that "diversity in education and gender" is positively correlated with innovation, thus "providing evidence on the importance of a diverse knowledge base among employees."[392]

---

391 Sylvia Ann Hewlett et al., "How Diversity Can Drive Innovation," *Harvard Business Review* (December 2013).

392 Christian R. Østergaard et al., "Does a Different View Create Something New? The Effect of Employee Diversity on Innovation," *Research Policy* 40 no. 3 (April 2011): 500–509.

For example, Dr. Freudenthal spent years researching and developing cardiac occluders during his medical residency in Germany, but it was not until returning to Bolivia that he found in Aymara culture a solution to a technical problem that had been eluding him.

7. SUSPEND ASSUMPTIONS ABOUT THE DIRECTION IN WHICH THE BENEFIT WILL RUN.

Multiple stories in this book suggest that when the arts and the sciences are brought together, the benefit can run in unexpected directions. Often, the resulting benefit is not unidirectional, moving solely from the artistic discipline to the scientific one or vice versa, but rather symbiotic.

For example, when choreographer Dana Tai Soon Burgess interviewed scientists in order to lay the research foundation for creating the dance *We Choose to Go to the Moon*, he found the voices of the scientists so compelling that he ultimately chose to incorporate their interviews into the audio track of the performance. In this case, what was originally intended to inform the scientific aspect of the project unexpectedly ended up becoming art.

When researchers incorporated visual body mapping and storytelling into patient education, not only did the body mapping workshops prove helpful in improving health literacy among patients and their communities, but the body maps themselves became collectible gallery artwork. In this case, too, what was intended to yield only a scientific benefit also created art.

Sometimes, when the sciences and the arts are harnessed together for the benefit of a particular community, the benefits spill over more broadly than anticipated. When Ebeling combined music and technology to make music more accessible to deaf individuals, he created a product that ended up generating enthusiasm not just among deaf users but also among hearing ones. What was intended to benefit one specific demographic turned out to appeal to a much broader one.

When scientists began collaborating with dancers for the Dance Your PhD contest, many discovered that setting a dance to scientific concepts was not just a good way to convey the nature of their work to a broader audience; it was also a good way for the scientists to think through their own work more effectively during the research process. What researchers thought would help others grasp their work, in fact, helped the researchers themselves better understand their work.

8. FOCUS ON THE "WHY."

"It's not about what; it's about why," said Dr. Hannah Schneider, the founder and music director of Oxford Alternative Orchestra, when I asked her what principle she would propose.

Schneider's advice echoed the message of Simon Sinek's popular TEDx Talk "How Great Leaders Inspire Action," in which Sinek argued that all of the world's inspiring leaders and organizations, whether they work on technological innovation or civil rights activism, "think, act, and communicate" from the "inside out," always starting with the "why" before moving to the "how" and then the "what." "People don't buy what you do; they buy why you do it" was the resounding refrain of Sinek's talk.[393]

Schneider fully acknowledged the need for purpose-based leadership. "An interdisciplinary project is going to have a lot of problems and going to be very complex in many aspects," she affirmed. She gave the example of her latest initiative, the CHRYSALIS Project, which draws together choreographers and dancers, composers and musicians, cinematographers and editors, and a funding organization. "All of those people have different goals," she said, and not only that, but "they have different languages" in which they think about success and their goals.

She explained that interdisciplinary collaboration on that scale is "too hard if your goal is a what, if your goal is a noun, if it is 'I want to do something cool that looks like x.'" On the other hand, "if you have a good enough reason, you can get everyone on board."

For Schneider and her CHRYSALIS Project team, "the mission of bringing hope through the genre of art and using that to bring hope to people" amid the desolation they were experiencing in the pandemic is what kept everything together. "At the end of the day, we come back to why we are doing that," she shared.

---

393 Simon Sinek, "How Great Leaders Inspire Action | Simon Sinek," TEDx Talks, September 28, 2009, YouTube video, 17:47.

Similarly, Shekerjian underlined in her book the importance of having a clear mission in creative endeavors, for the sake of unleashing the confidence necessary for innovation:

"What harnesses the idea of vision to the creative impulse is the notion that dreams unleash the imagination. And taking this one step further, where the dream addresses some greater good, there is an even stronger tendency to take risks and make the innovative leaps necessary to accomplish its goals. Limit yourself to your own private world and you've limited your creativity by worrying about how to protect what you've got and how to get what you're missing. Get yourself out of the way in pursuit of some greater good, in response to a strong pull of mission, and you've liberated the mind."[394]

---

394 Shekerjian, *Uncommon Genius: How Great Ideas Are Born*, 96.

CONCLUSION

I hope that, upon picking up this book, you were intrigued and uplifted by the inspiring stories it contains. I hope that now, upon finishing it, you see it as more than a simple collection of stories. I hope you see it as a path forward.

In writing the book, I had a lot of questions about how to best structure it. When I first started the writing process, I thought about dividing it up by discipline: one part about the arts containing chapters on different art forms, and one part about the sciences containing chapters on the various branches of science. However, I soon discovered that structuring my book that way was neither feasible nor reflective of its purpose.

As I gathered compelling stories about successful innovations combining the arts and the sciences, I found it impossible to compartmentalize them by discipline, because art and science were so deeply intertwined within them. It was not a matter of one primary discipline being supplemented or supported by an auxiliary one; they were truly enmeshed with one another.

Therefore, I chose to structure the book based on the main outcome of each interdisciplinary innovation. As a result, an overarching structure emerged that presented, part by part and chapter by chapter, each of the ways in which combining the arts and the sciences is advantageous.

As it turned out, a book featuring impactful innovations at the intersection of the arts and the sciences could not avoid becoming a book about how the arts and the sciences are better together.

The conclusions below mirror the takeaways in Parts I, II, and III of this book.

The sciences advance the arts:

- Technology expands possibilities for artistic creation.
- Technology expands arts access, thereby increasing arts appreciation and the broader arts dialogue—and redefining the artistic experience for everyone.

The arts advance the sciences:

- The arts help us visualize, interpret, and discuss dynamic and spatially complex scientific data.
- The arts help medical providers better serve their patients.

The arts and sciences combined help us to get at the heart of what makes us good humans:

- The arts plus technology make a powerful statement to a large audience about issues of societal significance.

- The arts plus the sciences help us cultivate and express awe at the physical and metaphysical aspects of the incredible universe in which we live.

Going forward, I hope you will seize the opportunity to treat others as holding pieces of a puzzle no one person, and no one discipline, can necessarily solve.

ACKNOWLEDGMENTS

———

First and foremost, I would like to extend particular gratitude to Georgetown University professor of entrepreneurship and Creator Institute founder Eric Koester, who first invited me to embark on the book-writing journey, and whose positive energy and enthusiasm inspired me to believe I would succeed in it.

I also offer many thanks to the entire New Degree Press team, especially the head of publishing Brian Bies, my developmental editor Jonathan Jordan of Wordobe Media, and my marketing and revisions editors Cynthia Tucker and Kim LaCoste, who kept me moving toward the finish line. Additional thanks go to my layout editor Alexander Pavlovich, the head of marketing and revisions Leila Summers, the rest of the editing team, my cover designer Gjorgji Pejkovski, and author coaches Kyra Ann Dawkins, Mackenzie Finklea, and Stephen Howard. Thank you to my fellow New Degree Press authors, especially those who practiced pre-order pitches, conducted author interviews, and exchanged early praise with me.

I am so grateful to everyone who pre-ordered my book. First among them are my father and mother, David and Laurie Yelle, who were my biggest supporters. I am fortunate that my mother provided thoughtful reviews and substantive suggestions for my manuscript, as did Dr. Alan Whiting and Dr. Amalia Gnanadesikan. I extend my thanks to each of you, as well as to other members of my family and friends who have known me just as long or nearly so: Frank and Christy Monahan, DM Hoyt and Heidi Smets, Sean Monahan and Lisa Holtmann, Gary and Patty Gertig, Sherri Estep, Isaac Estep, and Dr. Marie Loiselle. My thanks also go to my childhood friends and former classmates Isabel Gorgoroso, Sarah Wohl, Dr. Sophia Choukas-Bradley, Dr. Hemal Sampat, Carmel Arikat, and Dr. Alexandra Lamar; my fellow Hoyas Linda Santiago, Faraz Mohammadi, and Ty Pinkins; my colleagues Emily Wilson, Tom Lang, Sonya Reines-Djivanides, Dr. Anne Boyle, Aynoor Ismailova Ford, James Holt, and Harrison Gill; my fellow Center for Arabic Study Abroad alumni Hossameddine Abouzahr and Emily Drevets; my fellow LeadIN Core alumna Jeanette Gass; StartingBloc Fellows Leah Miller, Kelsey Krach, Kushaan Shah, Camila Payan, Leon Wang, and Brandon D.; and Sister Anne Marie Elizabeth. Many of you fit into more than one of the aforementioned categories, which is a testament to what wonderful individuals and communities I have in my life.

Thank you to the hard-working and creative individuals who granted me primary interviews, especially Dr. Hemal Sampat and Dr. Hannah Schneider. How marvelous it is that, when I want to learn more about the things that fascinate me the most, I have only to pick up my phone and connect with friends whose hearts are as warm as their minds are brilliant.

I am appreciative of the StartingBloc community's significant role in providing great impetus throughout the book-writing process. I thank the Los Angeles 2019 Institute organizers, mentors, volunteers, and incoming fellows for creating a space in which I gained renewed inspiration to dream and act boldly. Their enthusiastic response to my book pitch gave me the impetus to put in the work to turn my idea into a reality.

I would like to recognize executive coach and thought partner Paul Mosca—another StartingBloc Fellow—for giving the gift of his time and energy in researching communities, initiatives, and resources at the intersection of the arts and the sciences on my behalf. He unearthed so many treasures for me on this topic I had not discovered on my own, and he did so incredibly quickly.

Kat Short led me to insights about shaping my personal story in relation to my book through a storytelling learning circle in 2019. I am grateful to Kat for facilitating this experience, Martha Cavazos for managing the logistics of it, and the other StartingBloc Fellows who accompanied me as participants in it.

Thanks also go to Terri Sinclair, who guided me over the course of several months in thinking through many topics directly or indirectly related to the process of writing and marketing my book, and so much more. Once again, I have StartingBloc and its community of social innovation fellows to thank for providing the incredibly valuable gift of Terri's coaching to me.

Suzie Smyth of Endless Possibilities was also tremendously helpful in coaching me to draw together the various strands of my personal and professional identity and weave them into a coherent and compelling message about who I am and what I do well. As I discover where this book will lead me, thanks to Suzie, I am better equipped to seize the opportunity to steer my way along the journey.

I am grateful to everyone who helped form me into a writer: my parents, especially my mother; the dozens upon dozens of teachers and professors who have shaped my formal education; and the colleagues who recognized my talents and gave me free rein to develop my potential.

My fourth-grade teacher, Suzanne Kline, wrote in the illustrated book of original poetry I created for a long-term in-class assignment, "Don't forget to call me when a publishing company comes knocking on your door!" Those words left a lasting impression. Twenty-five years later, I have not forgotten them.

Emily Wilson, author of *From Boats to Board Feet: The Wilson Family of the Pacific Coast*, gave me the valuable opportunity to focus professionally on writing and research as a teenager alongside my dear friend Halley Fehner, who was one of the best models for a focused work ethic and attention to detail that I have seen among anyone at any age.

Dr. Kristen Brustad and Dr. Tarik El-Ariss, my master's thesis advisor and co-reader, refined the foundational skills I drew upon to write this book and guided me through my first endeavor to complete an intensive research and writing project. Few graduate students would likely describe their thesis-writing experience as one of the most enjoyable aspects of graduate school, but for me it was, since an advisor who truly takes that role to heart makes all the difference.

Dr. Perry, Meredith, and Joanna Ariel Skeath have my lasting gratitude for seeing me through the most challenging stretch of the book-writing process, and for supporting me in ways that go far beyond friendship. May their kindness and generosity be returned manifold.

Finally, I am glad to have had Pekoe and Daisey, Humane Rescue Alliance foster cats, act as cute and comforting companions in the days leading up to my manuscript submission.

BIBLIOGRAPHY

INTRODUCTION

"About MacArthur Fellows Program." MacArthur Foundation. Accessed November 17, 2020. https://www.macfound.org/programs/fellows/strategy/.

Bayles, David, and Ted Orland. *Art & Fear: Observations on the Perils (and Rewards) of Artmaking.* Santa Cruz: Image Continuum Press, 1993.

Creativity: From Potential to Realization. Edited by Robert. J. Sternberg, Elena L. Grigorenko, and Jerome L. Singer. Washington, DC: American Psychological Association, 2004.

Csikszentmihalyi, Mihaly. *Creativity: Flow and the Psychology of Discovery and Invention.* New York: Harper Perennial, 1996.

Epstein, David. *Range: Why Generalists Triumph in a Specialized World.* New York: Macmillan Publishers, 2019.

Gladwell, Malcom. *Outliers: The Story of Success*. New York: Little, Brown and Company, 2008.

Jobs, Steve. "Steve Jobs' 2005 Commencement Address." Commencement address. Stanford University. June 12, 2005. Stanford, CA. Transcript and YouTube video, 15:04. https://news.stanford.edu/2005/06/14/jobs-061505.

Le, Hai H., Monika Looney, Benjamin Strauss, Michael Bloodgood, and Antony M. Jose. "Tissue Homogeneity Requires Inhibition of Unequal Gene Silencing during Development." *Cell Biology* 241 no. 3 (2016): 319–331. https://doi.org/10.1083/jcb.201601050.

Malone, Thomas W., Robert Laubacher, and Tammy Johns. "The Big Idea: The Age of Hyperspecialization." *Harvard Business Review*, July–August 2011. https://hbr.org/2011/07/the-big-idea-the-age-of-hyperspecialization.

Martins, Katie M. "Vowel Terminology as a Method for Dating Early Arabic Grammatical Texts: A Case Study of Kitāb al-jumal fī l-naḥw." Master's thesis, University of Texas at Austin, 2014. https://repositories.lib.utexas.edu/handle/2152/26416.

Root-Bernstein, Robert, and Michele Root-Bernstein. "Artistic Scientists and Scientific Artists: The Link Between Polymathy and Creativity." *In Creativity: From Potential to Realization*, edited by Robert Sternberg, Elena Grigorenko, and Jerome Singer, 127–151. Washington, DC: American Psychological Association, 2004.

Shekerjian, Denise. *Uncommon Genius: How Great Ideas Are Born*. New York: Penguin Books, 1991.

Snow, C. P. "The Two Cultures." Lecture given at the University of Cambridge, Cambridge, United Kingdom, May 7, 1959. http://s-f-walker.org.uk/pubsebooks/2cultures/Rede-lecture-2-cultures.pdf.

CHAPTER 1: TECHNOLOGY INCREASES ARTS ACCESSIBILITY

"Avnet and Not Impossible Labs Enable the Deaf to Experience Live Music." Business Wire, September 25, 2018. Accessed August 24, 2020. https://www.businesswire.com/news/home/20180925005793/en/Avnet-Impossible-Labs-Enable-Deaf-Experience-Live.

Bukszpan, Daniel. "Zappos Wants the Deaf and Hard-of-Hearing to Listen to Music—Here Is the Technology for It." CNBC, October 23, 2018. Accessed August 24, 2020. https://www.cnbc.com/2018/10/23/here-is-how-zappos-is-helping-the-deaf-hear-concert-music.html.

"Didú. Touching the Prado." EstudiosDurero, September 6, 2016. YouTube video, 2:43. https://www.youtube.com/watch?v=3BysS4F2Imc&t=11s.

Hansen, Phil. "Embrace the Shake | Phil Hansen | TED Talks." TED, May 21, 2013. YouTube video, 10:02. https://www.youtube.com/watch?v=YrZTho_o_is&t=4s.

Hewitt, David. "Please Touch the Art: 3-D Printing Helps Visually Impaired Appreciate Paintings." Smithsonian Magazine, February 26, 2015. Accessed August 24, 2020. https://www.

smithsonianmag.com/innovation/please-touch-art-3-d-print-ing-helps-visually-impaired-appreciate-paintings-180954420/.

"The Museo del Prado, Visitors Numbers 2011." Museo del Prado, January 3, 2012. Accessed August 24, 2020. https://www. museodelprado.es/en/whats-on/new/the-museo-del-prado-visitors-numbers-2011/8cb6d8ac-9ec1-41b5-9f81-54b163f5f0f8.

Ouellete, Jennifer. "New Wearable Tech Lets Users Listen to Live Music through Their Skin." Ars Technica, November 25, 2018. Accessed August 24, 2020. https://arstechnica.com/gaming/2018/11/new-wearable-tech-lets-users-listen-to-live-music-through-their-skin/.

CHAPTER 2: THE TECHNOLOGY-ASSISTED CREATIVE PROCESS

Bayles, David, and Ted Orland. *Art & Fear: Observations on the Perils (and Rewards) of Artmaking.* Santa Cruz: Image Continuum Press, 1993.

Braga, Matthew. "The Verbasizer was David Bowie's 1995 Lyric-Writing Mac App." VICE, January 11, 2016. Accessed August 24, 2020. https://www.vice.com/en/article/xygxpn/the-verbasizer-was-david-bowies-1995-lyric-writing-mac-app.

Brooks, Katherine. "High-Tech Ballet Shoes Hypnotically Trace the Physical Movement of Dancers' Feet." HuffPost, November 17, 2014. Accessed October 10, 2020. https://www.huffpost.com/entry/lesia-trubat_n_6148618.

Carter, James. "Motion Bank Creates an Archive of Dancer's Movements." VICE, August 13, 2013. Accessed January 20, 2021. https://www.vice.com/en/article/wnpeyn/motion-bank-creates-an-archive-of-dancers-movements.

Dance Reality. Accessed January 20, 2021. https://www.dancerealityapp.com/.

"Dance Reality." AppTrace. Accessed February 16, 2021. https://www.apptrace.com/app/1277367395.

"David Bowie." Rock & Roll Hall of Fame. Accessed November 21, 2020. https://www.rockhall.com/inductees/david-bowie.

"How David Bowie Used 'Cut Ups' to Create Lyrics—BBC News." BBC News, January 11, 2016. YouTube video, 1:34. https://www.youtube.com/watch?v=6nlW4EbxTD8.

Inspirations. Directed by Michael Apted. 1997. Chicago: Home Vision Entertainment, 2002. DVD.

Kleon, Austin. "The Surprisingly Long History of the Cut-Up Technique." Austin Kleon (blog), September 18, 2018. Accessed November 21, 2020. https://austinkleon.com/2018/09/18/the-surprisingly-long-history-of-the-cut-up-technique/.

Skybetter, Sidney. "Meet the Choreographic Interface Designer Who Brings Her Dance Knowledge to Google." *Dance*, September 23, 2020. Accessed October 17, 2020. https://www.dancemagazine.com/interaction-design-2647573749.html.

Southern, Taryn. Taryn Southern. Accessed November 21, 2020.
https://www.tarynsouthern.com.

Southern, Taryn. Virtual "Creator Speaker Series" discussion with
Eric Koester hosted by the Creator Institute. November 11, 2020.

Sweeting, Adam. "David Bowie Obituary." *The Guardian*, January
11, 2016. Accessed November 21, 2020. https://www.theguardian.com/music/2016/jan/11/obituary-david-bowie.

Trubat, Lesia. "E-TRACES." Behance, November 6, 2014. Accessed
November 21, 2020. https://www.behance.net/gallery/21108721/
E-TRACES.

Walczak, Barbara. "Doubrovska's Class." *Ballet Review* 43 no. 3
(Fall 2015): 53–58. http://www.balletreview.com/images/Ballet_Review_43-3_Doubrovska.pdf.

CHAPTER 3: TECHNOLOGY FOR DEMOCRATIZATION OF THE ARTS

Fei, JiaJia. "Art in the Age of Instagram | Jia Jia Fei | TEDxMarthasVineyard." TEDx Talks, March 2, 2016. YouTube video, 13:23.
https://www.youtube.com/watch?v=8DLNFDQt8Pc.

Kaganskiy, Julia. "The Art Incubator: Julia Kaganskiy at New Inc."
April 19, 2018. In *State of the Art*. Produced by ART19. Podcast,
MP3 audio, 1:30:39. https://art19.com/shows/state-of-the-art/
episodes/e3c842ec-35f8-4b13-ad86-7e2fd0ec8d8f.

"New Paradigms and Spaces for Artistic Expression." Leonardo Art/Science Evening Rendezvous. Virtual presentation and discussion hosted by Stanford University, August 27, 2020.

Oviedo Clark, Astrid. "The World of Art: Navigating and Collecting in Today's Market." Virtual presentation and discussion hosted by Georgetown University, August 25, 2020.

Silver, Leigh. "Interview: Lindsay Howard Talks Curating the First Digital Art Auction with Phillips and Tumblr." Complex, October 10, 2013. Accessed October 4, 2020. https://www.complex.com/style/2013/10/lindsay-howard-paddles-on.

CHAPTER 4: ARTISTIC PRACTICES AS SCIENTIFIC ADVANCEMENTS

Aguirre, Edwin L. "Finding Inspiration in Origami and Eggshells." University of Massachusetts Lowell. October 15, 2019. Accessed September 7, 2020. https://www.uml.edu/engineering/research/engineering-solutions/origami-eggshells.aspx.

"The Amazing Origami of Robert Lang." Wired, June 26, 2008. YouTube video, 2:17. https://www.youtube.com/watch?v=xz-caYbSfkTs&t=1s.

An, Donghwy, and Nara Youn. "The Inspirational Power of Art on Creativity." Journal of Business Research 85 (April 2018): 467–475. https://doi.org/10.1016/j.jbusres.2017.10.025.

"Caltech Alumnus Manan Arya: Origami … in Space!" caltech, April 26, 2017. YouTube video, 3:39. https://www.youtube.com/watch?v=S-jlbx2x_Cg&t=1s.

Camci-Unal, Gulden, and Michelle A. Nguyen. "Reimagining Eggshells and Other Everyday Items to Grow Human Tissues and Organs." The Conversation, September 18, 2019. Accessed August 24, 2020. https://theconversation.com/reimagining-eggshells-and-other-everyday-items-to-grow-human-tissues-and-organs-123552.

de los Reyes, Ignacio. "The Bolivian Women Who Knit Parts for Hearts." BBC, March 29, 2015. Accessed August 31, 2020. https://www.bbc.com/news/health-32076070.

Feder, Toni. "Q&A: Robert Lang, Origami Master." Physics Today, January 8, 2018. Accessed September 7, 2020. https://physicstoday.scitation.org/do/10.1063/PT.6.4.20180108a/full/.

Freudenthal, Franz. "A New Way to Heal Hearts without Surgery | | Franz Freudenthal." TED, September 30, 2016. YouTube video, 9:28. Accessed August 24, 2020. https://www.youtube.com/watch?v=IYDqtxvKDW4&t=2s.

Heath, Alexandra, and Franz Freudenthal. "Weaving Solutions for the Heart." La Ciudad de las Ideas. 2016. Accessed August 31, 2020. https://ciudaddelasideas.com/en/videos/alexandra-heath-franz-freudenthal-cdi-2016-play-the-game/.

Heath, Alexandra, Inge von Alvensleben, Joaquin Navarro, Gabriel Echazú, Rainer Kozlik-Feldmann, and Franz Freudenthal. "Developing High Medical Technology, a Challenge for Developing Countries: The Percutaneous Closure of Atrial Septal Defects Using Nit-Occlud ASD-R: Early and Mid-term Results." World Journal for Pediatric and Congenital Heart Surgery 10 no. 4 (2019). https://doi.org/10.1177/2150135119845257.

"How NASA Engineers Use Origami to Design Future Spacecraft."
Seeker, March 25, 2018. YouTube video, 4:20. https://www.you-
tube.com/watch?v=Ly3hMBD4h5E&t=135s.

Jemison, Mae. "Mae Jemison on Teaching Arts and Sciences
Together." TED, May 5, 2009. YouTube video, 16:18. https://
www.youtube.com/watch?v=6VyoncmUvUw&t=1s.

Lang, Robert. "The Math and Magic of Origami | Robert Lang."
TED, July 31, 2008. YouTube video, 18:03. https://www.youtube.
com/watch?v=NYKcOFQCeno&t=611s.

"The Life-Saving Weaving of Bolivia's Indigenous Women." Great
Big Story, April 25, 2017. YouTube video, 3:03. https://www.you-
tube.com/watch?v=dHDDQVB2SnE&t=1s.

Martins, Alejandra. "Los inventos del médico boliviano que salvó
miles de niños." BBC, October 2, 2014. Accessed May 15, 2021.
https://www.bbc.com/mundo/noticias/2014/10/141002_med-
ico_boliviano_corazon_am.

Rodriguez, Joshua. "Flower Power: NASA Reveals Spring Starshade
Animation." National Aeronautics and Space Administration.
Accessed September 1, 2020.

"See a NASA Physicist's Incredible Origami." Great Big Story,
March 16, 2017. YouTube video, 3:00. https://www.youtube.
com/watch?v=DJ4hDppP_SQ.

CHAPTER 5: ART AIDS SCIENTIFIC THINKING

Abdullah, Makola. "STEM and the Arts | Dr. Makola Abdullah | TEDxRVA." TEDx Talks, May 26, 2016. YouTube video, 10:00. https://www.youtube.com/watch?v=MmboiJh6qJU.

Bohannon, John. "Dance vs. PowerPoint, a Modest Proposal—John Bohannon." TED-Ed, November 28, 2012. YouTube video, 11:17. https://www.youtube.com/watch?v=onqhopRhju4&t=1s.

Buehler, Markus. "Breaking the Wall of Matter and Sound: If a Virus Could Sing." Falling Walls. Accessed January 22, 2021. https://falling-walls.com/discover/videos/breaking-the-wall-of-matter-and-sound-if-a-virus-could-sing/.

Buehler, Markus J. "If A Virus Could Sing." Falling Walls. Accessed November 21, 2020. https://falling-walls.com/remote2020/finalists/breaking-the-wall-of-matter-and-sound-if-a-virus-could-sing/.

"Caltech Alumnus Manan Arya: Origami … in Space!" Caltech, April 26, 2017. YouTube video, 3:39. https://www.youtube.com/watch?v=S-jlbx2x_Cg&t=1s.

Chandler, David. "Vibrations of Coronavirus Proteins May Play a Role in Infection." Massachusetts Institute of Technology (MIT), November 19, 2020. Accessed November 21, 2020. https://news.mit.edu/2020/vibrations-coronavirus-proteins-1119.

"Flock Logic." Princeton University. Accessed September 29, 2020. http://www.princeton.edu/~flocklogic/.

Holtgrieve, Joseph. "The Lessons of Engineering Improv." *Inside Higher Ed*, January 11, 2018. Accessed August 29, 2020. https://www.insidehighered.com/views/2018/01/11/how-engineering-students-can-learn-through-improvisational-theater-opinion.

Hu, Yiwen, and Markus J. Buehler. "Comparative Analysis of Nanomechanical Features of Coronavirus Spike Proteins and Correlation with Lethality and Infection Rate." *Matter* 4 (January 16, 2021): 1–11. https://doi.org/10.1016/j.matt.2020.10.032.

Karp, Warren. "'Art and Science' OR 'Art or Science'? | Warren Karp | TEDxAugusta." TEDx Talks, March 7, 2016. YouTube video, 12:50. https://www.youtube.com/watch?v=WfpK8TZ-FldA&t=1s.

Leonard, Naomi E., George F. Young, Kelsey Hochgraf, Daniel T. Swain, Aaron Trippe, Willa Chen, Katherine Fitch, and Susan Marshall. "In the Dance Studio: An Art and Engineering Exploration of Human Flocking." Princeton University. Accessed September 29, 2020. http://www.princeton.edu/~naomi/publications/2014/flocklogicChapRevcol.pdf.

Loftus, Margaret. "Command Performance." *Prism*, May 2018. Accessed March 9, 2021. http://www.asee-prism.org/command-performance/.

Morris, Amanda. "Engineers Learn the Art of Allowing." Northwestern University, May 26, 2016. Accessed March 9, 2021. https://www.mccormick.northwestern.edu/news/articles/2016/05/engineers-learn-the-art-of-allowing.html.

"USDA Invests $4.8 Million in Three 1890 Centers of Excellence." US Department of Agriculture, June 3, 2020. Accessed March 8, 2021. https://www.usda.gov/media/press-releases/2020/06/03/usda-invests-48-million-three-1890-centers-excellence#:~:text=(Washington%2C%20D.C.%2C%20June%203,Land%2DGrant%20Institutions%20in%20America.

Venugopal, Vineeth. "Scientists Have Turned the Structure of the Coronavirus into Music." *Science*, April 3, 2020. Accessed August 24, 2020. https://www.sciencemag.org/news/2020/04/scientists-have-turned-structure-coronavirus-music#.

Willyard, Cassandra. "The Agony and Ecstasy of Cross-disciplinary Collaboration." *Science*, August 27, 2013. Accessed August 29, 2020. https://www.sciencemag.org/careers/2013/08/agony-and-ecstasy-cross-disciplinary-collaboration.

CHAPTER 6: ART AS STEM EDUCATION AND SCIENCE COMMUNICATION

Amit, Elinor, Caitlyn Hoeflin, Nada Hamzah, and Evelina Fedorenko. "An Asymmetrical Relationship between Verbal and Visual Thinking: Converging Evidence from Behavior and fMRI." *NeuroImage* 152 (2017): 619–627. https://doi.org/o.1016/j.neuroimage.2017.03.029.

Benington Weiss, Jackie. "Protein Synthesis: An Epic on the Cellular Level." *MATTERS OF ACT: A Journal of Ideas* 1 (Winter 2017): 52–53. https://issuu.com/alreadynotyet/docs/moa_a.

Bennett, Nichole. "STEMprov on Austin Public." Nichole Bennett, July 19, 2018. YouTube video, 7:47. https://www.youtube.com/watch?v=F1erduNmePY.

Bobek, Eliza, and Barbara Tversky. "Creating Visual Explanations Improves Learning," *Cognitive Research: Principles and Implications* 1 no. 1 (2016): 27. https://doi.org/10.1186/s41235-016-0031-6.

Bohannon, John. "The Winner of This Year's 'Dance Your Ph.D.' Contest Turned Physics into an Art." *Science*, February 15, 2019. Accessed August 29, 2020. https://www.sciencemag.org/news/2019/02/winner-year-s-dance-your-phd-contest-turned-physics-art.

"Dance of the Diagram." National Math Festival. Accessed November 21, 2020. https://www.nationalmathfestival.org/event/dance-of-the-diagram/.

"Differential Cohomology Documentary." Barkin/Selissen Project, June 13, 2017. YouTube video, 15:00. https://www.youtube.com/watch?v=y1I5BmJlFoo.

"Getting to Know Kyla Barkin." *Monkeyhouse*, January 17, 2014. Accessed September 29, 2020. http://conversingwithchoreographers.blogspot.com/2014/01/getting-to-know-kyla-barkin.html.

"Jacob's Pillow Dance 2012." Berkshire Fine Arts, June 7, 2012. Accessed November 21, 2020. https://www.berkshirefinearts.com/06-07-2012_jacob-s-pillow-dance-2012.htm.

Kayama, Ikumi. "The Art of Science and the Science of Art | Ikumi Kayama | TEDxFoggyBottom." TEDx Talks, May 6, 2015. YouTube video, 6:01. https://www.youtube.com/watch?v=cX8sq-JYjo6I&t=2s.

"Kyla Barkin and Aaron Selissen Present World Premiere of Differential Cohomology, New Dance Work Inspired by Mathematical Theory." *The Dance Enthusiast*, 2011. Accessed September 29, 2020. http://www.dance-enthusiast.com/dance-listings/events/view/Kyla-Barkin-and-Aaron-Selissen-Present-World-Premiere-of-Differential-Cohomology-New-Dance-Work-Inspired-by-Mathematical-Theory-.

Lux, Hal. "The Secret World of Jim Simons." *Institutional Investor Magazine*, November 1, 2000. Accessed September 29, 2020. https://faculty.fuqua.duke.edu/~charvey/Teaching/BA453_2005/II_On_Jim_.pdf.

"Nichole Bennett." LinkedIn. Accessed November 21, 2020. https://www.linkedin.com/in/bennettnichole/.

Patel, Kasha. Virtual Creator Speaker Series with Eric Koester hosted by the Creator Institute, October 14, 2020.

Roy, Sanjoy. "Dance+: Protein Synthesis—an Epic on the Cellular Level." *Springback Magazine*, August 11, 2020. Accessed September 26, 2020. https://springbackmagazine.com/read/dance-plus-protein-synthesis-epic-cellular-level/.

"Scientific Movement: The Art of Science and Dance." The Science & Entertainment Exchange. Accessed September 29, 2020.

http://scienceandentertainmentexchange.org/blog/scientific-movement-the-art-of-science-and-dance/.

Stimpson, Andrew Jay. "Axioms for Differential Cohomology" (PhD diss., Stony Brook University, 2011). https://dspace.suny-connect.suny.edu/handle/1951/56129.

Weiss, Gabriel. "Protein Synthesis: An Epic on the Cellular Level." Internet Archive, November 23, 2019. Accessed August 29, 2020. https://archive.org/details/ProteinSynthesis.

Young, Lauren. "In 1971, Stanford Students Did an Interpretive Dance to Demonstrate Protein Synthesis." Atlas Obscura, March 10, 2017. Accessed August 29, 2020. https://www.atlasobscura.com/articles/stanford-70s-interpretive-dance-protein-synthesis.

CHAPTER 7: ART FOR ENHANCED HEALTHCARE

Arntfield, Shannon L., Kristen Slesar, Jennifer Dickson, and Rita Charon. "Narrative Medicine as a Means of Training Medical Students toward Residency Competencies." *Patient Education and Counseling* 91 no. 3 (June 2013): 280–286. https://doi.org/10.1016/j.pec.2013.01.014.

Chambers, Sarah, and Julie Glickstein. "Making a Case for Narrative Competency in the Field of Fetal Cardiology." *Literature and Medicine* 29 no. 2 (Fall 2011): 376–395. https://doi.org/10.1353/lm.2011.0320.

Charon, Rita. "Honoring the Stories of Illness | Dr. Rita Charon | TEDxAtlanta." TEDx Talks, November 4, 2011. YouTube video, 18:16. https://www.youtube.com/watch?v=24kHX2H-tU30&t=455s.

Clark, Kevin, and Imen Maaroufi. "Point Motion: A Musical Tool, for Quantified Outcomes." Virtual presentation and discussion hosted by the Transformative Technology Community, October 15, 2020.

Encyclopaedia Britannica Online. Academic ed. s.v. "Apollo." Accessed October 3, 2020. https://www.britannica.com/topic/Apollo-Greek-mythology.

Encyclopaedia Britannica Online. Academic ed., s.v. "Music therapy." Accessed October 15, 2020. https://www.britannica.com/topic/music-therapy.

Fioretti, Chiara, Ketti Mazzocco, Silvia Riva, Serena Oliveri, Marianna Masiero, and Gabriella Pravettoni. "Research Studies on Patients' Illness Experience Using the Narrative Medicine Approach: A Systematic Review." *BMJ Open* 6 (2016). http://dx.doi.org/10.1136/bmjopen-2016-011220.

Garrison, David, Jeffrey Lyness, Julia Frank, and Ronald Epstein. "Qualitative Analysis of Medical Student Impressions of a Narrative Exercise in the Third-Year Psychiatry Clerkship." *Academic Medicine* 86 no. 1 (January 2011): 85–89. https://doi.org/10.1097/ACM.0b013e3181ff7a63.

Gastaldo, Denise, Natalia Rivas-Quarneti, and Lilian Magalhães. "Body-Map Storytelling as a Health Research Methodology: Blurred Lines Creating Clear Pictures." *Forum Qualitative*

Sozialforschung / Forum: Qualitative Social Research 19 no. 2, art. 3 (May 2018). http://dx.doi.org/10.17169/fqs-19.2.2858.

"Mapping Our Lives: Mapping Workshop Manual." University of Cape Town, April 2007. http://webcms.uct.ac.za/sites/default/files/image_tool/images/256/Mapping%20Our%20Lives%20Manual%20%20-%20April%202007.pdf.

McCloskey, Danielle. "An Interview with Danae Prosthetics' CEO Winston Frazer." *SciArt Magazine*, April 2018. Accessed August 24, 2020. https://www.sciartmagazine.com/spaces--places-danae-prosthetics.html.

Muszkat, Mordechai, Arie Ben Yehuda, Scott Moses, and Yaakov Naparstek. "Teaching Empathy through Poetry: A Clinically Based Model." *Medical Education* 44 (2010): 489–526. https://doi.org/10.1111/j.1365-2923.2010.03673.x.

"Narrative Medicine." Columbia University. Accessed September 24, 2020. http://sps.columbia.edu/narrative-medicine/.

Nowaczyk, Małgorzata J. M. "Narrative Medicine in Clinical Genetics Practice." *American Journal of Medical Genetics, Part A* 158A no. 8 (August 2012): 1941–1947. https://doi.org/10.1002/ajmg.a.35482.

Pearson, A. Scott, Michael P. McTigue, and John L. Tarpley. "Narrative Medicine in Surgical Education." *Journal of Surgical Education* 65 no. 2 (March–April 2008): 99–100. https://doi.org/10.1016/j.jsurg.2007.11.008.

Pitts, Jonathan M. "Baltimore Startup Blends Art and Technology in Helping Amputees Design Personalized Prosthetic Covers." *The Baltimore Sun*, April 6, 2018. Accessed September 24, 2020. https://www.baltimoresun.com/health/bs-hs-custom-prosthetic-covers-20180403-story.html.

Renzulli, Leigh Ann. "'Heart of the Harvey' Explores the Intersection of Art and Medicine." Georgetown University. April 3, 2016. Accessed October 3, 2020. https://gumc.georgetown.edu/gumc-stories/heart-of-the-harvey-explores-the-intersection-of-art-and-medicine/.

Samuel, Sigal. "This Doctor Is Taking Aim at our Broken Medical System, One Story at a Time." Vox, March 5, 2020. Accessed September 24, 2020. https://www.vox.com/the-highlight/2020/2/27/21152916/rita-charon-narrative-medicine-health-care.

Shekerjian, Denise. *Uncommon Genius: How Great Ideas Are Born*. New York: Penguin Books, 1991.

Shiel, Jr., William C. "Medical Definition of Hippocratic Oath." MedicineNet. Accessed November 14, 2020. https://www.medicinenet.com/hippocratic_oath/definition.htm.

"The Team." Point Motion. Accessed November 14, 2020. https://pointmotioncontrol.com/team/.

"Tech25." *Washington Life*, February 2019, 40. https://issuu.com/washingtonlife/docs/wlo219_digital/40.

"Visual Body Maps and 'Mapping Our Lives.'" University of Cape Town. Accessed September 24, 2020. http://www.cssr.uct.ac.za/cssr/asru/outreach/visualbodymaps.

Weiler, Lance. "'Creating a Clearing'—Dr. Rita Charon on the Power of Narrative Medicine." Medium, September 20, 2017. Accessed November 14, 2020. https://medium.com/columbia-dsl/creating-a-clearing-dr-rita-charon-on-the-power-of-narrative-medicine-e68befo5eb66.

Zambon, Kate. "Putting the Heart in 'The Heart of the Harvey.'" Georgetown University. April 9, 2017. Accessed August 31, 2020. https://gumc.georgetown.edu/gumc-stories/putting-the-heart-in-the-heart-of-the-harvey/.

Zambon, Kate. "Making Space for the Soul at the Heart of the Harvey." Georgetown University, April 16, 2018. Accessed August 31, 2020. https://gumc.georgetown.edu/gumc-stories/https://gumc.georgetown.edu/gumc-stories/making-space-for-the-soul-at-the-heart-of-the-harvey/.

CHAPTER 8: ART AS SCIENCE AND TECHNOLOGY ACTIVISM

Allahyari, Moreshin."Moreshin Allahyari: On Digital Colonialism, Re-figuring, and Monstrosity." UM Stamps, November 7, 2017. YouTube video, 59:12. https://www.youtube.com/watch?v=HcK9K4Yty74&t=1s.

Before It's Too Late. Accessed August 29, 2020. http://www.beforeitstoolate.earth/.

Before It's Too Late (@bitl.earth). Instagram account. https://www.instagram.com/bitl.earth/.

Eghan, Adizah. "Artist Uses 3D Tech to Recreate Past Destroyed by ISIS." KQED, January 14, 2016. Accessed August 29, 2020. https://www.kqed.org/arts/11228415/artist-uses-3d-tech-to-recreate-past-that-isis-destroyed#:~:text=At%20software%20company%20Autodesk%20at,the%203D%20printers%20are%20humming.&text=But%20resident%20artist%20Morehshin%20Allahyari,that's%20over%202%2C000%20years%20old.

Encyclopaedia Iranica Online. Academic ed., s.v. "Hatra." Accessed March 9, 2021. https://www.iranicaonline.org/articles/hatra.

Franklin-Wallis, Oliver. "Defying Daesh—with a 3D Printer." *Wired*, March 19, 2017. Accessed August 24, 2020. https://www.wired.co.uk/article/defying-daesh-with-a-3d-printer.

Jones, Christopher. "Assessment of the ISIS Destruction at the Mosul Museum." Ancient History Et Cetera, March 9, 2015. Accessed August 24, 2020. https://etc.ancient.eu/education/destruction-mosul-museum/.

Menendez, Alicia, and Lorna Baldwin. "In Miami, How Art Intersects with Technology and Climate Change." *PBS NewsHour*, May 29, 2019. Accessed August 24, 2020. https://www.pbs.org/newshour/show/in-miami-how-art-intersects-with-technology-and-climate-change#transcript.

Milbrandt, Melody K. "Understanding the Role of Art in Social Movements and Transformation." *Journal of Art for Life* 1

no. 1 (Spring 2010): 7–18. https://journals.flvc.org/jafl/article/
view/84087.

Neill, Alex. "Art and Emotion." In *The Oxford Handbook of Aesthetics*, edited by Jerrold Levinson, 421–435. Oxford: Oxford University Press, 2003.

CHAPTER 9: ART AND SCIENCE CULTIVATE AWE

Anderson, Angela. "Art Draws Out the Beauty of Physics." *Symmetry*, April 12, 2016. Accessed November 14, 2020. https://www.symmetrymagazine.org/article/art-draws-out-the-beauty-of-physics.

Arcangeli, Margherita, Marco Sperduti, Amélie Jacquot, Pascale Piolino, and Jérôme Dokic. "Awe and the Experience of the Sublime: A Complex Relationship." *Frontiers in Psychology* 11 (2020): 1340. https://doi.org/10.3389/fpsyg.2020.01340.

"The Art and Science of Awe." Greater Good Science Center. Accessed March 6, 2021. https://ggsc.berkeley.edu/what_we_do/event/the_art_and_science_of_awe.

Codik, Emily. "Dana Tai Soon Burgess Premieres Fluency in Four in Tribute to His Late Father." *Washingtonian*, September 11, 2015. Accessed August 24, 2020. https://www.washingtonian.com/2015/09/11/dana-tai-soon-burgess-premieres-fluency-in-four-in-tribute-to-his-late-father/.

Csikszentmihalyi, Mihaly. *Creativity: Flow and the Psychology of Discovery and Invention*. New York: Harper Perennial, 1996.

Dana Tai Soon Burgess Dance Company. Accessed November 14, 2020. http://dtsbdc.org/dtsbdc/.

Dawson, Victoria. "A Dancer and a Scientist Deliver a New Take on the Moon Walk." *Smithsonian Magazine*, September 14, 2015. Accessed August 24, 2020. https://www.smithsonianmag.com/smithsonian-institution/dancer-and-scientist-deliver-new-take-moon-walk-180956590/.

Feynman, Richard P. *"Surely You're Joking, Mr. Feynman!" Adventures of a Curious Character*. New York: W. W. Norton & Company, 1997.

Freeman, Jameson. "Serendipity." *Self-Center* (blog), December 14, 2018. http://blog.jameson.live/2018/.

Gottlieb, Sara, Dacher Keltner, and Tania Lombrozo. "Awe as a Scientific Emotion." *Cognitive Science* 42 no. 6 (2018). https://doi.org/10.1111/cogs.12648.

"Interview with Our Artistic Director." The CHRYSALIS Project, January 28, 2021. YouTube video, 4:47. https://www.youtube.com/watch?v=JMrvtS_Mq4E.

Kaufman, Sarah. "Burgess at 20: Dance Fully Evolved." *The Washington Post*, September 23, 2012. Accessed August 24, 2020. https://www.washingtonpost.com/lifestyle/style/burgess-at-20-dance-fully-evolved/2012/09/23/140bfb60-05a5-11e2-a10c-fa5a255a9258_story.html.

Kaufman, Sarah L. "Dana Tai Soon Burgess Dancers Cosmically Intertwine Art and Science." *The Washington Post*,

September 20, 2015. Accessed October 13, 2019. https://
www.washingtonpost.com/entertainment/theater_dance/
the-ties-that-bind-are-seen-as-oily-in-four-works-by-da-
na-tai-soon-burgess/2015/09/20/f598f2b8-5fca-11e5-b38e-
06883aacba64_story.html.

Kennedy, John F. "We Choose to Go to the Moon." Recorded at
Rice University in Houston, Texas, September 12, 1962. https://
er.jsc.nasa.gov/seh/ricetalk.htm.

Kim, James S. "Over the Moon with Dana Tai Soon Burgess."
Character Media, August 29, 2015. Accessed August 24, 2020.
https://charactermedia.com/over-the-moon-with-dana-tai-
soon-burgess/.

Lee, Sydney. "Professor Brings the Space Race to the Stage in
Dance Show at the National Portrait Gallery." *The GW Hatchet*,
December 15, 2018. Accessed August 29, 2020. https://www.
gwhatchet.com/2018/12/15/professor-brings-the-space-race-
to-the-stage-in-dance-show-at-the-national-portrait-gallery/.

McLaughlin, Jeff. *The Originals: Classic Readings in Western Philosophy*. Victoria, BC: BCcampus/TRU, 2017. https://pressbooks.
bccampus.ca/classicreadings/.

O'Brien, Jane. "NASA Collaborates on Interpretive Dance about
Space." BBC, October 7, 2015. Accessed November 24, 2020.
https://www.bbc.com/news/av/entertainment-arts-34461735.

Perlin, Joshua D., and Leon Li. "Why Does Awe Have Prosocial
Effects? New Perspectives on Awe and the Small Self." *Per-*

spectives on Psychological Science 15 no. 2 (2020). https://doi. org/10.1177/1745691619886006.

Shekerjian, Denise. *Uncommon Genius: How Great Ideas Are Born.* New York: Penguin Books, 1991.

Stellar, Jennifer. "How Culture Shapes the Experience of Awe." *Greater Good Magazine.* Accessed March 6, 2021. https:// greatergood.berkeley.edu/video/item/how_culture_shapes_ the_experience_of_awe.

Stellar, Jennifer E., Neha John-Henderson, Craig L. Anderson, Amie M. Gordon, Galen D. McNeil, and Dacher Keltner. "Positive Affect and Markers of Inflammation: Discrete Positive Emotions Predict Lower Levels of Inflammatory Cytokines." *Emotion* 15 no. 2 (2015): 129–133. https://doi.org/10.1037/ emo0000033.

"What Is Awe?" *Greater Good Magazine.* Accessed March 6, 2021. https://greatergood.berkeley.edu/topic/awe/definition.

CHAPTER 10: THE CASE FOR INTERDISCIPLINARITY

Appiah, Kwame Anthony. "What Is the Point of College?" *The New York Times Magazine*, September 13, 2015. Accessed March 8, 2021. https://www.nytimes.com/2015/09/13/magazine/what-is-the-point-of-college.html.

Ayuob, Nasra N., Basem S. Eldeek, Lana A. Alshawa, and Abdulrahman F. ALsaba. "Interdisciplinary Integration of the CVS Module and Its Effect on Faculty and Student Satisfaction as

Well as Student Performance." *BMC Medical Education* 12 no. 50 (2012). https://doi.org/10.1186/1472-6920-12-50.

Blackwell, Alan F., Lee Wilson, Charles Boulton, and John Knell. *Radical Innovation: Crossing Knowledge Boundaries with Interdisciplinary Teams*. Cambridge: University of Cambridge Computer Laboratory, 2009. https://www.cl.cam.ac.uk/techreports/ UCAM-CL-TR-760.pdf.

Bras, Rafael L., Ari W. Epstein, Kip Vernon Hodges, and Alberta Lipson. "Students' Perceptions of Terrascope, A Project-Based Freshman Learning Community." *Journal of Science Education and Technology* 16 no. 4 (2007): 349–364. http://hdl.handle. net/1721.1/49458.

Caruso, Denise, and Diana Rhoten. "Lead, Follow, Get Out of the Way: Sidestepping the Barriers to Effective Practice of Interdisciplinarity." The Hybrid Vigor Institute, 2011. http://citeseerx. ist.psu.edu/viewdoc/download?doi=10.1.1.130.5143&rep=rep1& type=pdf.

"Colleges Facing Cuts to Arts and Humanities Programs." College Art Association of America, November 8, 2018. Accessed March 10, 2021. http://www.collegeart.org/news/2018/11/08/ colleges-facing-cuts-to-arts-and-humanities/.

Epstein, David. *Range: Why Generalists Triumph in a Specialized World*. New York: Macmillan Publishers, 2019.

Filippou, Filippos, Stella Rokka, Athena Pitsi, Dimitrios Gargalianos, Evangelos Bebetsos, and Dafni-Anastasia Filippou. "Interdisciplinary Greek Traditional Dance Course: Impact on Student Satisfaction and Anxiety." *International Journal of Instruction* 11 no. 3 (2018): 363–374. https://eric.ed.gov/?id=EJ1183437.

Fischer, Karin. "In Rhode Island, an Unusual Marriage of Engineering and Languages Lures Students." *The Chronicle*, May 18, 2012. Accessed March 8, 2021. https://www.chronicle.com/article/in-rhode-island-an-unusual-marriage-of-engineering-and-languages-lures-students/?bc_nonce=ioq47fmmqgreyfc45381ct&cid=reg_wall_signup.

"The Future of Jobs 2020." World Economic Forum, October 20, 2020. https://www.weforum.org/reports/the-future-of-jobs-report-2020.

Ghanbari, Sheena. "Learning Across Disciplines: A Collective Case Study of Two University Programs That Integrate the Arts with STEM." *International Journal of Education and the Arts* 16 no. 7 (2015). https://files.eric.ed.gov/fulltext/EJ1069829.pdf.

Hediger, Viktor, Solveigh Hieronimus, Julia Klier, and Jörg Schubert. "Closing the Future-Skills Gap." McKinsey, January 29, 2019. Accessed September 24, 2020. https://www.mckinsey.com/industries/public-and-social-sector/our-insights/closing-the-future-skills-gap#.

Herstatt, Cornelius, and Katharina Kalogerakis. "How to Use Analogies for Breakthrough Innovations." *International Journal of Innovation and Technology Management* 2 no. 3 (2005): 331–347. https://doi.org/10.1142/S0219877005000538.

Jiang, Lin, Brent Clark, and Daniel Turban. "Creating Break-throughs: The Role of Interdisciplinary Idea Networking and Organizational Contexts." *Academy of Management Proceedings* no. 1 (2015): 18645. https://doi.org/10.5465/ambpp.2015.176.

Klein, Julie Thompson. *Creating Interdisciplinary Campus Cultures: A Model for Strength and Sustainability.* San Francisco: John Wiley & Sons, 2009.

Mullin, Rick. "Behind the Scenes at the STEM–Humanities Culture War." *Chemical & Engineering News* 97 no. 29 (July 16, 2019). https://cen.acs.org/education/undergraduate-education/Behind-the-scenes-STEM-humanities-culture-war/97/i29.

Nissani, Moti. "Fruits, Salads, and Smoothies: A Working Definition of Interdisciplinarity." *Journal of Educational Thought* 29 no. 2 (August 1995): 121–128. http://www.jstor.org/stable/23767672.

Olds, Barbara M., and Ronald L. Miller. "The Effect of a First-Year Integrated Engineering Curriculum on Graduation Rates and Student Satisfaction: A Longitudinal Study." *Journal of Engineering Education* 93 no. 1 (2004): 23–35. https://doi.org/10.1002/j.2168-9830.2004.tb00785.x.

Oskam, I. F. "T-Shaped Engineers for Interdisciplinary Innovation: An Attractive Perspective for Young People as Well as a Must for Innovative Organisations." *37th Annual Conference—Attracting Students in Engineering,* Rotterdam, The Netherlands, vol. 14 (2009): 1–10. https://www.researchgate.net/profile/Inge-Oskam/publication/216353140_T-shaped_engineers_for_interdisciplinary_innovation_an_attractive_perspective_for_young_

people_as_well_as_a_must_for_innovative_organisations/
links/0046353c6d3a468771000000/T-shaped-engineers-for-
interdisciplinary-innovation-an-attractive-perspective-for-
young-people-as-well-as-a-must-for-innovative-organisations.
pdf.

"Preparing Technicians for the Future of Work." National Science
Foundation. Accessed November 14, 2020. https://www.pre-
paringtechnicians.org/.

Shamir, Lior. "A Case against the STEM Rush." *Inside Higher
Ed*, February 3, 2020. Accessed March 10, 2021. https://www.
insidehighered.com/views/2020/02/03/computer-scientist-urg-
es-more-support-humanities-opinion.

Stewart-Gambino, Hannah, and Jenn Stroud Rossman. "Often
Asserted, Rarely Measured: The Value of Integrating Humanities, STEM, and Arts in Undergraduate Learning." The
National Academies of Sciences, Engineering, and Medicine
(2015). https://sites.nationalacademies.org/cs/groups/pgasite/
documents/webpage/pga_170985.pdf.

CHAPTER 11: EIGHT PRINCIPLES OF INTERDISCIPLINARY INNOVATION

Biello, David. "Fact or Fiction?: Archimedes Coined the Term
'Eureka!' in the Bath." *Scientific American*, December 8, 2006.
Accessed March 5, 20201. https://www.scientificamerican.com/
article/fact-or-fiction-archimede/.

Csikszentmihalyi, Mihaly. *Creativity: Flow and the Psychology of
Discovery and invention*. New York: Harper Perennial, 1996.

Epstein, David. *Range: Why Generalists Triumph in a Specialized World*. New York: Macmillan Publishers, 2019.

Hewlett, Sylvia Ann, Melinda Marshall, and Laura Sherbin. "How Diversity Can Drive Innovation." *Harvard Business Review*, December 2013. https://static1.squarespace.com/static/5ae89190aa49a17d6e450047/t/5b0d92c4aa4a99c9a42dd d3c/1527616197302/How+Diversity+Can+Drive+Innovation+_ HBR.pdf.

Knapp, Bernhard, Rémi Bardenet, Miguel O. Bernabeu, Rafel Bordas, Maria Bruna, Ben Calderhead, Jonathan Cooper, Alexander G. Fletcher, Derek Groen, Bram Kuijper, Joanna Lewis, Greg McInerny, Timo Minssen, James Osborne, Verena Paulitschke, Joe Pitt-Francis, Jelena Todoric, Christian A. Yates, David Gavaghan, and Charlotte M. Deane. "Ten Simple Rules for a Successful Cross-Disciplinary Collaboration." *PLOS Computational Biology* 11 no. 4 (April 30, 2015): e1004214. https:// doi.org/10.1371/journal.pcbi.1004214.

"New Paradigms and Spaces for Artistic Expression." Leonardo Art/Science Evening Rendezvous. Virtual presentation and discussion hosted by Stanford University, August 27, 2020.

Østergaard, Christian R., Bram Timmermans, and Kari Kristinsson. "Does a Different View Create Something New? The Effect of Employee Diversity on Innovation." *Research Policy* 40 no. 3 (April 2011): 500–509. https://doi.org/10.1016/j.respol.2010.11.004.

Shekerjian, Denise. *Uncommon Genius: How Great Ideas Are Born*. New York: Penguin Books, 1991.

Sinek, Simon. "How Great Leaders Inspire Action | Simon Sinek."
TEDx Talks, September 28, 2009. YouTube video, 17:47. https://
www.youtube.com/watch?v=u4ZoJKF_VuA.

Made in the USA
Middletown, DE
26 June 2021